Real and Relevant

Real and Relevant

A Guide for Service and Project-Based Learning

Katy Farber

ROWMAN & LITTLEFIELD
Lanham • Boulder • New York • London

Published by Rowman & Littlefield
A wholly owned subsidiary of The Rowman & Littlefield Publishing Group, Inc.
4501 Forbes Boulevard, Suite 200, Lanham, Maryland 20706
www.rowman.com

Unit A, Whitacre Mews, 26-34 Stannary Street, London SE11 4AB

Copyright © 2017 by Katy Farber

British Library Cataloguing in Publication Information Available

Library of Congress Cataloging-in-Publication Data

978-1-4758-3544-1 (cloth : alk. paper)
978-1-4758-3545-8 (pbk. : alk. paper)
978-1-4758-3546-5 (electronic)

♾ ™ The paper used in this publication meets the minimum requirements of American National Standard for Information Sciences Permanence of Paper for Printed Library Materials, ANSI/NISO Z39.48-1992.

Printed in the United States of America

To my brother Mike, for always believing in me.

Contents

Growing World Changers

Our future leaders
will need to solve
vexing problems
finding sustainable energy
ending hunger
how to live peacefully
stop disease
heal food systems
grow habitats
and more than
I could name
in one poem

What makes us think
that listening
and doing worksheets
will create people
who can save the world?

They need to question
They need to plan
They need to argue
They need to rehearse
and then they need to call
leaders and experts

Themselves

They need to debate
to analyze
and finally decide

what to do
and then do it

NOW

They need to see connections
opposing perspectives
listen with grace and respect
but then counter argue
and make their point
eloquently
with examples
from history

We become not
teachers on a stage
but facilitators
mediators
cheerleaders
truth seekers
questioners
reflection makers
and joyful learners

Witnesses
of hope
potential
and our future

This is education
This is teaching
This is learning
That makes a difference
and changes the world
—Katy Farber

Preface

Be the change you wish to see in the world. —Ghandi

My entry into service learning was not easy or peaceful. When asked what teacher would be crazy enough to lead fifty fifth- and sixth-grade students in a service-learning project that would be videotaped and made into a film for teachers and students, my principal said "Katy Farber." So there I was, leading students in brainstorming questions about our local watershed, with a microphone on my shirt and a video camera shining a light in my face.

I had led smaller service-learning projects before and had some successes and many challenges. It was after several years of different kids, projects, problems, assessments, community partners, and mentors that I truly felt comfortable with this kind of untraditional, innovative learning.

I've always been idealistic about teaching, thinking that small groups of people could change the world, make a difference, and foster deep learning along the way. This is what service learning does. It turns students into problem solvers, critical thinkers, and experimenters—not just receptacles for our knowledge.

My students have located and preserved habitats, built community gardens, set up school composting and recycling programs, created numerous field guides, written and illustrated children's books with science themes, and created and performed plays to teach younger students about science, history, and culture. Did they learn what the district, state, and nation said they had to? You bet, and so much more. They learned that they matter in the world, that they can cause change, ask questions, solve problems, get help, and work together to make a difference in their school, community, and world.

This book is a guide for busy, hardworking teachers to start using service learning and project-based learning as a teaching tool, or to extend and enrich what they are already doing. The book is also for environmental educators, childcare providers, afterschool program providers, and others interested in pursuing innovative, life-changing service-learning projects with youth. It is my hope that you find it clear, concise, easy to use, motivating, and disarming as you plan your units and lessons in any subject. Service learning has energized my teaching, and it is my hope that it will for you, too. There are many student benefits in service learning that you will read about, but one benefit that is often overlooked is how it can change the way you look at teaching. Witnessing children learning this way gives me hope for the future. Watch your students teach, shine, explore, ask, lead, change, and discover, and eventually, change the world for the better. You will feel the difference.

Now that I have moved on to leading teachers in project- and service-based learning, my commitment to the practice has only grown stronger. I have conducted new research about the power of service learning with early adolescents, which I will share more about in this book, and have seen how this type of learning engages kids across the spectrum of students, grades K–12. We are on the cusp of great educational change—with our students leading the way. We can engage and excite students by exploring their interests and community problems through integrated, meaningful, and relevant projects like they will face in the real world. It is my deepest hope that you find this book helpful to your practice.

Acknowledgments

I want to thank Martin Kemple of Foodworks and community member John Puleio for first encouraging me to begin using service learning as a teaching tool many years ago. From these two I learned how to lead these kinds of projects, and how to connect with the community in meaningful ways. I also want to thank special educator Julie Smart and Farm to School Organizer for Shelburne Farms Dana Hudson for their stellar editing, which went well beyond the bounds of normal friendship. A big thank-you to my students at Rumney Memorial School, who taught me the power and beauty of service learning. To all of my colleagues at the Tarrant Institute of Innovative Education at the University of Vermont, thank you for inspiring and challenging me to be my best every day. I could not be blessed with a better team to help schools innovate in a time of massive educational change. To all of the teachers I currently work with—you are leading the charge. Your commitment to your students, to your profession, and to improving our communities is just what we need in the world. I cannot thank you enough for being willing to partner with me (and TIIE) in this important work.

You give me hope for the future.

Introduction

This book, updated to a new edition in 2017, is a guide to help new and experienced teachers across the country make the leap into creating and leading service and project-based learning with their students. Many teachers are already doing this meaningful and important work. I hope that if you are, you will find ways to deepen, further explore, or assist in your work by reading this book.

If you are just starting out with service and project-based learning, I hope this book provides you with relevant information, from teacher to teacher, to make this kind of learning doable in your busy teaching life. This book is for new teachers, experienced teachers, teachers in nontraditional settings as well as public and private schools, grades 3–12, across all subject areas. The new edition features new chapters on project-based learning, new research about how service learning meets middle school students' developmental needs, additional resources, and updated information, and expands to include project-based learning and new examples from the field, including information about Makerspaces, Genius Hours, and passion projects.

Real and Relevant: A Guide for Service and Project-Based Learning is not a philosophy book filled with ideals and educational jargon. It is a guide with concepts broken down into chapters that seemed the most useful to me, after leading service learning with my students for almost twenty years.

By engaging in service or project-based learning with your students, you are doing nothing less than changing the world for the better. By letting your students explore and begin to solve real-life problems, they acquire deeper knowledge, new skills, newfound motivation, responsibility, and engagement. The data support this, but the real joy is seeing this happen with your own students.

In chapter 1, service learning is defined and contrasted with community service. Often these concepts are confused, and clarification and definitions help to demonstrate what service learning is all about. Chapter 2 is about the similarities and differences between service and project-based learning. Chapter 3 focuses on the many benefits of service learning, from academic to social and personal; the positive effects of service learning are wide reaching. My new research is the basis for the fourth chapter about service learning at the middle school level.

How to build a strong community to set the stage for service and project-based learning is the focus of chapter 5. Chapter 6 will guide you to gather ideas with your students for service-learning projects in your content area and grade levels. A process for guiding your students from brainstorming to a focused question is part of this chapter as well. Planning for the project is the focus of chapter 7. Teachers are given ideas and tips for how to plan each important step for creating, completing, and sharing service-learning projects. Partnering with the community during service-learning projects is the topic for chapter 8.

Teachers know that working in teams can yield wonderful learning experiences but can also be a challenge. Chapter 9 will explore how the team might progress through a service-learning project, and troubleshoot challenging or difficult situations. How to assess service-learning projects is the focus of chapter 10. Many examples of rubrics, checklists, and alternative assessments are shared in this chapter. Chapter 11 will show how to develop reflection activities for students to deepen and enrich service and project-based learning experiences.

Funding is a challenge for everyone these days, especially schools. Chapter 12 will explore resources for how to fund your service-learning projects, in straightforward and manageable ways. Technology tools that can help with project-based and service learning will be described in chapter 13. New projects and programs that can utilize aspects of service and project-based learning, including Makerspaces, Genius Hour, and Passion Projects, are featured in chapter 14. Chapter 15 shares five interviews with creative and dynamic teachers who are currently leading service or project-based learning with their classes. Many tips, ideas, and rays of inspiration are to be found in these interviews.

At the end of every chapter, there is a resource section. There is a great wealth of information on the web and in print about service learning. These sections will point you to the most valuable ones within a certain topic. Also, many chapters include an appendix with ready-to-use (or adapt to your needs) teaching resources for service and project-based learning. These are meant to be immediately useful for teachers.

On the whole, I hope *Real and Relevant* provides teachers with a realistic, integrated, and inspirational guide for how to lead service and project-based learning with your students. Feel free to adapt, adjust, and use whatever you can from this book to help you as you change the world with service and project-based learning!

Chapter One

What Is Service Learning?

Talk does not cook rice. —Chinese proverb

Service learning is not a new idea. Teachers across the country, for most of the nineteenth century, have been linking the needs of the community with learning in their classrooms. In fact, it was John Dewey who was a fervent early supporter of service learning. He "believed that students would learn more effectively and become better citizens if they engaged in service to the community and had this service incorporated into their academic curriculum" (NCES, 2010). And that was in 1916! He was way ahead of his time in this (and many other) areas.

So we can see the early roots of service learning, but it did not really gain educational traction until the 1970s. Cognitive psychologists such as Lev Vygotsky and Jerome Bruner pointed out that "learning involves the creation of meaning and is highly individualized," and that service learning provides an opportunity for developing relevant and meaningful ways to learn about abstract and often challenging concepts (University of Southern California, 2010). Then in the 1990s, legislation and support for service learning blossomed.

In the years of 1990–1999, many reforms to support and extend community-based learning were put in place, such as the National and Community Service Act of 1990, through the Serve America program, and the National and Community Service Trust Act of 1993, through the Learn and Serve America program, provided support for service-learning activities in elementary and secondary schools (Corporation for National Service, 1999). In addition, through programs such as AmeriCorps, the federal government has offered opportunities to high school graduates, college students, and recent college graduates to serve local communities in exchange for stipends and

1

payment of education loans or money toward future postsecondary education. Both Learn and Serve America and AmeriCorps are administered by the Corporation for National Service, a federal organization also created by the National and Community Service Trust Act of 1993 (NCES, 2010).

Throughout the 2000s, we saw growth in service learning across the country, with some states requiring it for all students.

> For half a century, service-learning has spread in American schools. In the last decade, it was spurred to new growth by congressional and presidential actions and funding. In increasing numbers, schools have provided service-learning opportunities for students that connect their curriculum studies to activities such as tutoring younger children, adopting a river, creating a museum exhibit, or conducting oral histories with senior citizens. In these and similar instructional activities, youth have simultaneously learned to serve and served to learn. They are becoming both better students and better citizens. (National Commission on Service Learning, 2010)

With the election of Barack Obama in 2008, a renewed sense of service has been infused in the spirit of our nation and citizenry. With all the development of service-oriented activities in the classroom, there has been a growth of interest in community service and service learning in classroom settings. But there have also been lots of misunderstanding as to what is meant by these terms and how they might ultimately benefit students the most.

If you ask a teacher or parent what service learning is, you'll probably hear them say, "Oh, community service? Our school does that. We have a food drive every year."

While this is wonderful, it is not service learning. There is a lot of confusion about what it really is, and how it is much more than community service. Service learning is not meant to take the place of community service projects that schools are involved in. And it is not simply calling community service by a new name. Community service is extremely valuable and important to schools, communities, families, and individuals. But there are many meaningful differences between the two concepts.

COMMUNITY SERVICE

Let's start by looking at community service. Traditionally community service targets a local or global need or raises money for a cause. The cause and event are usually chosen and led by adults, with support from students and families.

The beneficiary could be a neighbor, or an Amazon rainforest thousands of miles away. Usually this is a finite event, taking up a day, weekend, or few weeks.

Examples of community service are:

- food drives, or other collections for charity;
- hospital visits;
- UNICEF or other non-profit support;
- nursing home visits;
- animal shelter visits;
- cleaning a park or habitat;
- picking up litter;
- helping out at a local library; or
- assisting children or people with learning or physical disabilities.

Community service often benefits a local community, nonprofit organization, or group in need. It is practiced by people to connect and volunteer in their local communities, to fulfill school, business, or extracurricular requirements, or at times as a punishment.

Community service may be mandatory, part of a community or court process, or part of a graduation requirement. It generally does not include specific learning objectives or organized reflection and extension opportunities. Community service activities can be a single event, a short series, or regular engagement completed in schools, community groups, or clubs.

You've experienced these before and have a good sense of what community service is and looks like. These activities are meaningful and valuable but are usually led and coordinated by adults, and are finite in duration.

HOW SERVICE LEARNING IS DIFFERENT

Service learning is a learning tool to empower students to solve problems in their own communities, or even globally. It is a student-driven process, where students learn about a particular issue, place, or problem, then figure out how to take action in a positive way. Then they actually do it. Students themselves (with teacher guidance) do research, make calls, write letters, and solve problems. Ultimately they share this process with their schools, families, and communities, and that is where the real change happens.

Service learning takes time. It can't be an add-on to a curriculum. It has to be embedded and integrated for it to work with busy teachers and a full curriculum. Service learning is all about the process: It builds in reflection, takes weeks or months, and culminates in a community celebration. Community service is a piece of this process. In short, community service is "the action" in isolation.

According to Learn and Serve America's National Service Learning Clearinghouse: "Service-Learning is a teaching and learning strategy that integrates meaningful community service with instruction and reflection to enrich the learning experience, teach civic responsibility, and strengthen communities" (NSLC, 2010).

A service-learning nonprofit called KIDS Consortium supplies professional development, grants, and resources to teachers completing service-learning projects with their classes. Their definition of service learning is: "A method of teaching/learning that challenges students to identify, research, propose, and implement solutions to real needs in their school community as part of their curriculum" (KIDS Consortium, 2005).

So while there is crossover, and a definite need for both community service and service learning, there are real and distinct differences. This book is about how to lead, plan, organize, and assess meaningful service-learning projects with your students. Teachers will find that service learning enriches, extends, and enlivens community service in great measure.

This quotes sums up the difference between the two concepts:

> We define community service as volunteering in the community for some form of extrinsic reward, such as fulfilling a graduation requirement or obtaining class credit. Service learning, in contrast, is a teaching method that combines academic content with direct service experiences in which students provide genuine service to their school or community while extending or deepening their understanding of curricular content. (Hopkins, 2008)

SCHOOLS LOOKING TO CONNECT MORE WITH COMMUNITIES

More and more schools across America now have some sort of service as a regular part of the school experience. According to the National Center of Education Statistics in 1999,

- 64 percent of all public schools, including 83 percent of public high schools, had students participating in community service activities recognized by and/or arranged through the school; this increased to 68 percent in 2008 (NCES, 2008).
- 57 percent of all public schools organized community service activities for their students.

For these schools, community service is already happening and with some training and planning, more service learning could take place that would net even more positive results for student and the community. Learning could be extended in rich and meaningful ways by developing service-learning projects in these schools.

Schools are interested in developing problem-solving, critical-thinking students who can handle the challenges of our rapidly changing society.

> About one-fifth (19 percent) of schools with service-learning said that one of their top 3 reasons for encouraging student involvement in service-learning were to teach critical thinking and problem solving skills. In addition, 12 percent of schools with service learning said that improving student achievement in core academic courses was one of their most important reasons for encouraging student involvement in service-learning. (NCES, 2010)

Clearly, schools across the United States are using service as a way to help students improve their academic achievement, and as they do, they are discovering benefits in multiple areas of student achievement and success, as you will see in the upcoming chapter.

Specifically, service learning has these components, many of which community service and community-based learning do not.

- Service learning is connected to the curriculum or will meet curricular goals (including grade-level or grade-cluster expectations).
- Community contacts and partnerships are created and fostered, exposing children to community members in real and meaningful ways.
- There is significant student choice in the topic area, project design, and focus.
- There is built-in reflection, so students are constantly thinking about their learning and projects.
- Students work in their communities to solve real-life problems.
- Students are assessed throughout the project in numerous ways.

Now here we are in 2017, and project-based learning has been growing across the nation. We will take a close look at project-based learning and how it differs from service learning in chapter 2. Service learning as an approach has continued to grow, especially in the university setting. Where it lags is middle school, even as this age group is developmentally a great fit for this work (more on that in chapter 4). For now, let's look at some examples of service learning to clarify this learning approach.

EXAMPLES OF SERVICE-LEARNING PROJECTS

- Rural Vermont fifth- and sixth-graders studying sustainability search through school trash and discover that students aren't recycling. In committees, students research recyclable items and trash and recycling companies, and work with a local nonprofit to secure recycling bins for the school. Then they teach the school community how and what to recycle, reducing school cost for trash collection and reducing the school's environmental footprint.

- "Elementary children in Florida studied the consequences of natural disasters. The class designed a kit for families to use to collect their important papers in case of evacuation with a checklist, tips about rescuing pets, and other advice to make a difficult situation easier, which students distributed to community members." (National Service Learning Clearinghouse, 2010)
- "Middle school students in Pennsylvania learned about the health consequences of poor nutrition and lack of exercise, and then brought their learning to life by conducting health fairs, creating a healthy cookbook, and opening a fresh fruit and vegetable stand for the school and community." (National Service Learning Clearinghouse, 2010)
- New York City elementary students noticed an ugly, abandoned lot near to their school. They fundraised and organized with community groups to develop a community garden space. (National Service Learning Clearinghouse, 2010)
- In one high school, a student died. The school was devastated, and put this energy into creating a memory garden for students who passed away. Students worked with the community sponsors and landscape architects to create a beautiful and meaningful space for the community.

Textbox 1.1
  Service learning is *not*:

- an add-on, another new thing to do in education;
- a one-time volunteer experience;
- only for older students;
- only for science or civics classes; or
- only for middle- and upper-class students.

In conclusion, this quote demonstrates the difference between service learning and community service with a clear example:

> If school students collect trash out of an urban streambed, they are providing a service to the community as volunteers; a service that is highly valued and important. On the other hand, when school students collect trash from an urban streambed, then analyze what they found and possible sources so they can share the results with residents of the neighborhood along with suggestions for reducing pollution, they are engaging in service-learning. (National Service Learning Clearinghouse, 2010)

The learning is enriched and extended through service learning in ways that just aren't possible with community service. Service learning is not a new idea. It does not have to be an add-on. Every teacher can make service learning work within his or her grade levels, content areas, and curriculum.

RESOURCES

National Service Learning Clearinghouse, www.servicelearning.org/what-service-learning. Great introductory article about service learning, and all around information-packed website.

KIDS as Planners: A Guide to Strengthening Students, Schools and Communities through Service Learning. KIDS Consortium Site, www.kidsconsortium.org.

The Complete Guide to Learning through Community Service: Grades K–9, by Lillian S. Stephens. This hands-on guide to implementing service learning provides information on planning projects, including hundreds of across-the-curriculum tie-in activities, sample projects, forms, questionnaires, and more.

Chapter Two

Project-Based Learning and Service Learning

What's What?

Education is not the filling of a pail; it is the lighting of a fire. —William Butler Yeats

If you are a practicing teacher, you likely have heard of project-based learning. Many schools are starting to use this approach to learning. Project-based learning has emerged in recent years as an engaging pedagogical tool that has many research benefits (Edutopia, 2016). It is of course rooted in constructivism and a type of teaching and learning that has been around for a long time. Dewey, known as the father of experiential learning, claims that all education is from experience (2007).

Several theorists extended Dewey's view that students learn from experience and hands-on social learning. These include Kolb (1984) and Vygotsky (1997), who noted how the teachers' role in authentic education shifts from an all-knowing stance, termed the banking method (Freire, 1970), to a role of facilitator and fellow problem solver. In other words, teachers do not simply fill students with their knowledge, but help them discover knowledge through their own experiences, reflections, and social interactions.

It can also re-invigorate teaching by creating exciting, real-life, integrated learning environments that ignite engagement in students—often ones who were not successful in traditional educational environments. Students and teachers want to feel that their work matters, that there is a greater meaning to it. Project-based and service learning give students relevance for their learning because it is rooted in their own communities and helping to solve complex problems. Let's first explore the meaning of *project-based learning*.

WHAT IS PROJECT-BASED LEARNING?

How do we solve problems in the real world? We use all of our resources. We research. We seek out solutions. We collaborate with others to devise a plan or design. We gather feedback and improve the idea, product, or outcome. Then we decide how we will share our ideas in the world.

This is the essence of project-based learning. Students take a real problem or issue, explore it in teams, develop a product and/or solution, or presentation, and share it to an authentic, engaged audience.

Like many terms in education, there are different definitions of *project-based learning*. Essentially, project-based learning breaks down into these steps:

1. A driving question.
2. An entry event.
3. Teams of students researching and developing a product or presentations.
4. Frequent reflection.
5. An authentic culminating event where students share their work to a relevant audience.

Let's take these one by one and explore what they mean.

DRIVING QUESTION

We will start with the driving question. This is critical to project-based learning. The driving question can come from very clear learning expectations required by the Common Core, proficiencies, or state standards. Or it can come from the students themselves. Essentially, it is a high-interest question linked to curricular goals. It can be in any subject. It's important that the question connects to students' experiences and that it can inspire students to improve their communities.

Here are a few examples:

- What impact has the Vermont Marble Company historically had on the town of Proctor, Vermont? How can that impact be felt today?
- How can we protect Vermont forests from invasive species?
- What challenges does each climate zone in the United States face and how can we help?

- How do idling cars impact the air quality at our school?
- What can we do to increase girls' access to education worldwide?
- How can we lessen our school's environmental footprint?

The driving question is the guide for the whole project-based learning unit. It is an anchor for the entire project, and teachers need to circle back to it frequently. It is important for questions to be open ended, invite inquiry, and leave lots of room for exploration. According to Edutopia (2016), driving questions should:

- tie into learning standards, proficiencies, or other district goals and expectations;
- address a real-world problem that relates to the students' experiences and community both in the school and out; and
- inspire students to find a solution that will have a long-lasting impact on their community.

It helps to collaborate on the driving question. You can ask for feedback from your teaching team or your students, or even co-create the question with your class. This helps to facilitate investment in the project as well as choice and voice. Once you have a driving question, it is time to move on to planning the entry event.

ENTRY EVENT

An entry event is just another label for what teachers have been doing for years: exciting students with an engaging opening event. Entry events are usually thought of during the planning stages of project-based learning. Sometimes they are the inspiration for the project. Other times they are brainstormed during the planning. Here are some ideas for entry events that can excite and motivate students (Farber, 2016a).

Take a Field Trip and Ask a Question

We know students are often inspired when they are outside of the school's walls and out in a different setting. For an exciting entry event, take students someplace outside the classroom, into the community, and ask them a challenging question. Ask them to consider something that might never have occurred to them, such as, "What would the community do if this resource were not here, or were unusable?" Or, "What is happening here? What do you notice?" At a historical site, you could ask, "How could our community engage more with this place?" Or at a landfill you could ask, "What will happen when this landfill is full?" Challenge your students with questions while they are in the field. Keep a list of their questions, comments, and ideas.

One example is when the students at Proctor Elementary School, in Proctor, Vermont, kicked off their project-based learning unit by visiting a local television station. This was an entry event to their project-based learning unit on extreme weather. Students researched extreme weather conditions and prepared virtual weather reports using a green screen, so they were very excited to see behind the scenes of how the station researches and produces their weather reports for broadcast.

Field trips can be real world or virtual. You can create an exciting entry event now by never leaving the classroom, but leaving virtually. Many historical sites and natural areas have virtual tours and websites that make exploring a place and asking questions available to all, no matter your school's resources. You could also take students on a virtual reality tour of an important place via Google Expedition or other technology tool (these will be discussed more in chapter 13). There are also so many thought-provoking videos now on YouTube and TeacherTube that can be used to get students thinking.

Do Something Dramatic

An entry event can also be some theatrics in your classroom. Many teachers love to do something unexpected and surprising for students. Examples include spreading out a tarp and dumping out your class's trash for all to see. How many recyclables are in there? How many compostables? More ideas include "cutting" electricity and connectivity to your classroom for a class period to kick off a study about renewable energy.

Or do some role-playing: stage a scenario with another teacher. One teacher did this to illustrate the concept of what a dictator is and how they can rise to power. He had a partner teacher come in and start giving orders—which students could sit where, which students benefited more than others, what colors they could wear. This certainly got a reaction from students! Simulations, role-plays, and kits are perfect for entry events and can get students excited and thinking differently about a topic.

Bring Current Events into the Classroom

Teachers can find a news article about a problem in your community you are thinking of exploring or basing your project-based learning around. Or you can find and share a compelling personal story about a national or international issue that could be the entry event, such as a first-person account of being a refugee, a girl without access to education, or other pressing national or local issue.

Does your community have an expert in the project-based learning topic area? You can ask that person to come speak with or present to your class on their area of expertise. Everyone loves being asked to share their knowledge and ideas, and this can create a powerful bond between your class and the community.

Picture Books

For the younger classes, selecting an exciting read-aloud book that launches into a discussion and project might be just the right fit. Thought-provoking books such as *The Lorax* or *The Sneetches* by Dr. Seuss can provide just the right frame and context for project-based learning with younger classes. Or picture books that develop empathy and perspective taking such as *The Table Where the Rich Kids Sit* by Byrd Baylor or *Fly Away Home* by Eve Bunting can build empathy and spark ideas for action.

Make an Event Out of a Compelling Image

Yes, it is true. Sometimes a photo is worth a thousand words. Many websites and social media accounts use photos to tell a compelling story that can be used as an entry event. The Humans of New York website and social media accounts capture the essence of so many New Yorkers and the American story (Humans of New York, 2016).

A similar project could be done in any town—in your town, or even your school.

For instance, for a project-based learning unit on community storytelling or history, make an entry event out of having your students take each other's photos and write fifty words describing the thing they most want everyone to know about them. Create a gallery from your photo stories displayed in a prominent place in the classroom. This can also be done about members of your school community and town. Students can be turned into photojournalists and take photos and oral histories of local community members. These can then be shared in a book, website, or other way with the community.

STUDENT RESEARCH

The next phase of project-based learning is students doing research. Depending on the age of the students, they might need significant support in this area. In appendix 2.1, you will find a sample portfolio, which helps students highlight important information found during research. You might need to modify or extend these resources. Often, during this phase some meaningful instruction can happen either teacher to students, or students to students. Topics can include:

- How to find a trustworthy online source
- What plagiarism is, and how to paraphrase
- How to take notes
- Primary and secondary sources
- How to cite a website
- Writing an outline of information
- Copyrighted images versus Creative Commons

Some teachers curate resources for students and provide them on a website or other sharing tool, then have the students visit only those sites for information. Some also provide very clear graphic organizers to help student gather important information. Resources for helping students gather information digitally will be explored in chapter 13.

REFLECTION

Reflection is an often-overlooked but critical part of both project-based and service learning. It is easy to leave out time for reflection in project-based learning because there are just so many other exciting things happening. The students are engaged, and it's fun and hands-on, and everything moves pretty quickly. But for project-based learning to connect to learning targets and goals, frequent reflection needs to happen, and it has to be deliberately built into the schedule.

Reflection in project-based and service learning is often where the big learning happens. Dewey wrote, "We do not learn from experience. We learn from reflecting on experience" (Dewey, 2007). So what are we looking for in a reflection?

The University of Minnesota (2016) encourages an exploration of these three questions: What happened? So what? And now what? Students can do this in many different ways, ranging from quick snapshot responses to longer, more involved reflections. Both are important and should be sprinkled into project-based learning units. Below, find some examples of reflection activities with students (Farber, 2016b).

Exit Tickets

Exit tickets are a powerful form of reflection and formative assessment. They can be a simple as a note card where a student quickly responds to a prompt. The prompt can be content-based, such as drawing an equilateral triangle, to assessing how your group is working as a team (or not). You can also use the exit ticket to have students constantly reflecting back to the driving question. If done regularly, you'll get to see progress over time.

Journals

This tried-and-true method of reflection is a very effective tool that can be used for a regular reflection activity. Weekly during project-based learning, students can answer questions such as:

• What have you learned about yourself as a learner this week?
• How can you connect what you are learning to your life?
• What new questions do you have based on your work this week?

A lot of project-based learning work is grounded in or draws from a strong STEM background. If this holds true for your project-based learning project, think about presenting the journal idea as a "lab notebook": what pieces of data do you want learners to capture, and more importantly, what do you want them to learn from that data?

Journals can also work nicely with simulation activities in project-based learning, such as role-playing, reenactments, or character perspective taking.

Videos

Video can be a powerful tool for reflection. Students can reflect in the form of a short video that they take themselves on a Chromebook, or iPod, or with their own devices. You can supply the prompt and students can start talking and recording. This also can work with audio for podcast creations.

Artwork

Reflection is not only the written word. It is easy to get stuck into thinking reflection has to be paragraphs and pages of text. Students can create a sketch or other piece of art that reflects their feelings, new learning, and how the group work is going. All modes of art can work for this purpose. Students can represent different aspects of the work both metaphorically (older students) and literally with sketches, painting, collages, or digital art.

Blogging

Students can write blog posts about their weekly project-based learning work and include videos, pictures, and links to sites and their work. This can become part of a portfolio and can build over time, showing progress and evidence of learning. It also can serve as formative instruction and can communicate about the project with parents.

Technology Tools for Reflection

There are so many great tech tools that can showcase student reflection. Tools like Wordle can turn concepts into interesting shapes, and Thinglink uses a photograph that can illustrate a concept with embedded links. Padlet can show brainstormed or linked topics, and students can make mind maps in Coogle or Prezi. Present some of these technology tools to your students for them to reflect, and they will likely be more excited than if they were to use a more frequent reflection tool—the journal.

These are just some tools for building reflection into project-based learning. Reflection doesn't have to be overwhelming, but it does have to be mindfully planned into both service and project-based learning. Hopefully, some of these ideas will work for your classroom and students.

CULMINATING EVENT

A culminating event is the public presentation of student work for the school and community. This can take many forms and doesn't have to be intimidating and scary for teachers and students. It does, however, have to provide a meaningful and authentic audience for students, which can give them the focus and motivation to do their very best work.

So what are culminating events? They can take many forms. These can include:

- *Exhibitions and presentations of student work.* These are for anyone beyond the teacher and the students who has a direct connection to the topic and work. These can include other students, school staff, members of the community, or specific groups around a topic, such as the school board, nonprofit organizations, town councils, policy makers, or others in the field. This can be in real time or virtually as well. Examples include presentations to the school board about how to save energy costs at the school, presenting survey findings of community members to a town council about how to improve the town, or presentations at a local museum about new student-created displays or resources.
- *Public sharing.* With so many digital sharing tools, students can create something of value in their project-based learning projects to share with the wider world. These can include educational YouTube videos, online maps, blog posts, or online magazines and websites.
- *Events.* These can be forums, dinners, talks, poetry slams, public readings, film festivals, learning festivals, game nights, math nights, tech nights, plays—any special event created and prepared for in the project-based learning process.

- *Create and share something.* These can include creating class books, chapters, public installations of art, models or sculptures, gardens, chicken coops, solar water heaters—the sky is the limit!

Culminating events are best thought of and planned before embarking on a project-based learning unit. Because they take a little planning, it is good to get this date on a project-based learning calendar or planning document (more on that later). Be sure to leave room in the schedule for students to practice and get feedback before any sharing. For younger students and first-time project-based learning teachers—start simple and small. A parent-sharing event might be the perfect culminating event for the first project-based learning unit.

HOW DOES PROJECT-BASED LEARNING DIFFER FROM SERVICE LEARNING?

Project-based learning and service learning are very similar. In service learning, service is an integral part of the learning. Service that mutually benefits both parties is essential. The service is not isolated or othering; rather, it is an experience that benefits everyone.

In project-based learning, there may or may not be a service component. There is a public presentation of the work, but not necessarily a service part of the work. Some student groups might have a service as part of the project-based learning that makes sense and is a key part of their project (such as building a garden for the community, creating a website for the town), and others might have a less service-oriented approach (such as a mock debate or design challenge).

In other words, service learning and project-based learning are close relatives. They are both incredibly motivating, dynamic, and transformative practices for teaching and learning. It is okay for teachers and students to move between these approaches, as long as each are done with fidelity, rigor, and careful planning. In terms of this guide, it can be used for both project-based and service learning.

PROJECT OR PROJECT-BASED LEARNING?

The Buck Institute of Education has some great resources about understanding the difference between projects and project-based learning. Essentially, they ask us to consider the following: Is the project the main dish or the dessert of the learning? Is the project itself the learning? Then it is project-based learning. Is the project a fun, short activity at the end of the unit? Then it is a dessert project.

Project-based learning also differs from projects because the projects are centered on a driving question, are collaborative, and change with student interest, community partners, and focus. Projects can be the same year after year, can have engaging hands-on parts, but are the same in terms of the end product. These are some differences between projects and project-based learning.

RESOURCES FOR PLANNING
A PROJECT-BASED LEARNING UNIT

As you can see, there is a lot to project-based learning. The work for the teacher is often heavily in the planning of the project, then facilitating the project with students. Thankfully, there are many planning resources to help you plan for project-based learning.

In appendix 2.1, you will find a planning template based on my experience, the Buck Institute's resources, and resources from Edutopia. Also, you can find a very helpful planning template from the Buck Institute here: http://tiie.w3.uvm.edu/blog/planning-a-pbl-unit/#.WEGqO6IrLYI.

This is only a one-chapter overview of project-based learning. If your interest is sparked, please read on, but also be sure to grab a copy of *Setting the Standard for Project-Based Learning* by John Larmer, John Mergendoller, and Suzie Boss (2015). This book is full of helpful ideas for how to launch, create, and manage project-based learning in your classroom.

RESOURCES

Project-based learning planning templates, http://tiie.w3.uvm.edu/blog/planning-a-pbl-unit/#.WEGtsqIrLYI.

Project-based learning series of blog posts from Tarrant Institute for Innovative Education, http://tiie.w3.uvm.edu/blog/category/ideas-for-educators/project-based-learning/#.WGe6vrYrln0.

Edutopia project-based learning resources, www.edutopia.org/project-based-learning.

Buck Institute for education website, packed with project-based learning resources, www.bie.org.

Chapter Three

Why Do Service Learning with Your Students

Research Review

I hear and I forget. I see and I remember. I do and I understand. —Chinese proverb

You might be a teacher wondering why you would want to guide students through a process like this when you can just arrange the details for them yourself, more quickly and efficiently. Or you might be wondering how this will work in your particular situation and if it would really benefit your students.

The short answer is: it will benefit them, immensely, in myriad ways, and potentially for a very long time.

This chapter will outline some of the many benefits of service learning to all students. The numbers and information here are critically important. Students benefit academically and socially, with personal and civic responsibility. And with 70 percent of schools doing some sort of service learning and community service, the successes seen from engaging in service learning for some students can make all the difference (National Center for Education Statistics, 1999). At the end of the chapter, I will share my new research on service learning's impact on middle-level students in particular.

STANDARDIZED TESTING GAINS

Teachers and schools have been mandated to do more standardized testing in schools than ever. High-stakes testing, for better (and for worse), is here to stay, and often is considered a measure of success for schools. This is debat-able, as far as success goes, but it is our current reality.

So when your disbelieving principal asks you why you want to do service learning, or the skeptical superintendent, or parent, you can proudly say that service learning raises standardized test scores. It also improves important lifelong skills, such as civic responsibility and engagement, but we will get to those later on in this chapter. Service and project-based learning increases test scores, but also says, "We are more than a test." You might also want to use the principal discussion guide I provide in appendix 2.1.

Individual schools and districts have been studying the effects of service learning in their districts on standardized tests. From increased participation and engagement, students are performing better on these state assessments.

> Service-learning helps academic improvement and higher order thinking skills.
>
>   Research shows that when service-learning is designed in particular ways, students show gains on measures of academic achievement, including standardized tests. The academic benefits of service-learning come when teachers explicitly tie service activities to standards and learning objectives, and when they design instruction that maximizes learning. Service-learning that includes environmental activities often yields student gains in the content areas of math (e.g., measurement and problem solving) and science (e.g., prediction and knowledge of botany) if these knowledge and skill areas are explicitly woven into the experience. In addition to acquisition of core knowledge and skills, some researchers found that many service-learning tasks help students to improve higher order thinking skills such as analysis, problem solving, decision-making, cognitive complexity, and inferential comprehension because they are exposed to relevant tasks that require them to use these types of skills. This benefit can be realized if teachers play an active role in facilitating dialogue and understanding of more complex tasks. (National Service Learning Clearinghouse, 2008)

Two states have found gains in particular curricular areas.

- "The Michigan study also revealed that service-learning students in the fifth grade demonstrated significantly higher test scores on the state assessment than their nonparticipating peers in the areas of writing, total social studies, and three social studies strands: historical perspective, geographic perspective, and inquiry/decision-making. No other statistically significant differences were found. The two aspects of service-learning that were most closely associated with positive results were linkage with curriculum and direct contact with those being served." (Billig, 2004)
- In Indiana, service-learning experiences improved standardized tests in both third and tenth grade. "Some schools have documented increased student scores on state standardized testing due to their participation in

service-learning projects. For example, in Paoli, Indiana, service-learning has been a part of the curriculum since 1994. This year, only four high school students failed one portion of the ISTEP. Roger Fisher, Assistant Superintendent for Paoli Community School Corporation, attributes the impressive results, in part, to a desire to attend school and learn that is fueled by their participation in service-learning. He estimates that all members of this year's graduating class will have participated in at least one service-learning project. The Education Commission for the States notes that this phenomenon is taking place nation wide. (Morgan, 1999)

According to researchers on the effects of service learning and standardized tests: "It appears that when high quality service-learning is intentionally tied to academics, participation can make a difference on standardized tests" (Billig, 2004).

The key to this success is projects that are intentionally linked to the curriculum, deepening and extending knowledge.

More and more, standardized tests, and life in general, are calling on students to solve critical-thinking, in-depth, real-life problems. Word problems that have multiple parts and complex, multifaceted solutions can be less overwhelming when students are considering problems like these within their own communities and regularly in their school's curriculum. Confidence is built from successful experiences, and this translates to more confidence in a test-taking environment.

Alfie Kohn, an educational researcher and author, often talks about the backward approach with "failing schools." When students aren't performing well, often schools will go back to basics, drilling students for limited chunks of information, often without much student thinking or logic expected or practiced. Students are also exposed to a more standardized reading curriculum, with a focus on scripted reading programs that a teacher merely follows. Alfie Kohn describes this phenomenon quite well:

> Often, of course, they can succeed in raising average test scores. You deprive kids of recess, eliminate music and the arts, cut back the class meetings and discussions of current events, offer less time to read books for pleasure, squeeze out the field trips and interdisciplinary projects and high-quality electives, spend enough time teaching test-taking tricks, and, you bet, it's possible to raise the scores. But that result is meaningless at best. When a school or district reports better test results this year than last, knowledgeable parents and other observers respond by saying, "So what?" (because higher test scores do not necessarily reflect higher quality teaching and learning)—or even, "Uh oh" (because higher test scores may indicate lower quality teaching and learning).
>
> And once you realize that the tests are unreliable indicators of quality, then what possible reason would there be to subject kids—usually African American and Latino kids—to those mind-numbing, spirit-killing, regimented

instructional programs that were designed principally to raise test scores? If your only argument in favor of such a program is that it improves results on deeply flawed tests, you haven't offered any real argument at all. Knock out the artificial supports propping up "Success for All," "Open Court," "Reading Mastery," and other prefabricated exercises in drilling kids to produce right answers (often without any understanding), and these programs will then collapse of their own dead weight. (Kohn, 2002)

What then lacks, in the setting Kohn describes, is the developing ability of students to solve complex and real-life problems. When reforming schools to promote academic success and boost test scores, educational leaders should not simply rely on route memorization, drills, and scripted programs. They should incorporate service learning in equal measure to give students exposure to this type of in-depth, integrated learning. Raising test scores in and of itself is not the answer, as Mr. Kohn points out—it is raising them while developing our students' critical thinking and real-world problem-solving skills.

IMPROVED GPA AND ATTENDANCE

Many studies have linked service learning with improved GPA and attendance records of students. When so many students are disconnected and disenfranchised with schools and learning, service learning can provide meaning and motivation for students to show up and care about their work. This lends itself to more success in all subjects, by increasing attendance and motivation.

This trend seems particularly powerful for students with risk factors against achieving academic success. According to the article "Fifteen Effective Strategies for Improving Student Attendance and Truancy Prevention," by Jay Smink and Mary S. Reimer: "Studies of the effects of service-learning on grades, attendance, and dropout reduction indicate the value of this strategy for student who have significant risk factors" (Smink & Reimer, 2004, p. 156).

There has been significant data to support the effects of improved attendance and GPA on students involved in service learning. Read on for more survey information from the Civic Enterprises that is quite striking in its support of service learning:

The Potential to Increase Student Attendance and Engagement

- 82 percent of students who participate in service-learning, and 80 percent of at-risk students not in service-learning programs, say their feelings about attending high school became or would become more positive as a result of service-learning. In focus groups, teachers highlighted the value of service-learning in increasing school and classroom attendance, and other studies have shown that high quality service-learning programs have a significant impact on student attendance.

- Other research shows that service-learning can help increase students' self-confidence, leadership skills, and sense of empowerment.
- Secondary research shows that service-learning can improve academic performance by improving test scores, homework completion, and grades, and can reduce the achievement gap between minority and majority students. Teachers explained in the focus groups that service-learning especially helps those who are not best served by the traditional classroom environment.
- Other studies also show that service-learning can improve student behavior, refocusing the school environment on learning while reducing the distractions caused by disruptive behavior. (Bridgeland, DiIulio, & Wulsin, 2008)

Students find a voice and passion that is not present in "normal" school through service learning. One student said, "Service-learning makes me want to come to school, because it's not the same thing all the time" (Bridgeland, DiIulio, & Wulsin, 2008). Amen to that. Service-learning projects are different day to day, week to week, project to project, based on the student groups, the focus, the teachers and community leaders, and school settings. Students thrive with this real-life, complex problem solving, and it more closely resembles the problems and opportunities they will encounter as adults. They show up more, and that is half the battle in the areas of improved academic achievement.

REDUCED DROPOUT RATES

Even more than merely showing up and being more involved is the idea that students are more likely to stay in school the more they are involved in service learning. How powerful this is: service learning can profoundly affect the success of a student's life—by impacting their decision to stay in school.

Service learning is quickly becoming a learning tool to prevent students from dropping out of school. Again from the report "Engaged for Success: Service Learning as a Tool for Dropout Prevention":

> Making Service-Learning More Widely Available
> as a Dropout Prevention Tool
> Service-learning alone cannot solve the complex problem of high school dropouts, but it can be a powerful tool to help address many of the warning signs that signal students are on track to leave school—absenteeism, lack of motivation, lack of engagement in classroom learning, and lack of connection to real-world opportunities. Students themselves believe service-learning would be a powerful tool to prevent high school dropout and want more access to service-learning opportunities.

- Seventy-four percent of African Americans, 70 percent of Hispanics, and 64 percent of all students said that service-learning could have a big effect on keeping dropouts in school. More than half of all at-risk students (53%) believed that service-learning could have this effect.
- Eighty-three percent of all students, 90 percent of African Americans, 83 percent of Hispanics, and 81 percent of whites, said they would definitely or probably enroll in service-learning classes if they were offered at their school. (Bridgeland, DiIulio, & Wulsin, 2008)

When considering the motivation of young people to stay in school, despite challenges and serious risk factors, one high school dropout put it succinctly in the report *The Silent Epidemic: Perspectives of High School Dropouts.*

> One bright young woman who was a leader in her focus group said: "If they related to me more and understand that at that point in time, my life was . . . what I was going through, where I lived, where I came from. Who knows? That book might have been in my book bag. I might have bought a book bag and done some work."
>
> Eighty-one percent of survey respondents said that if schools provided opportunities for real-world learning (internships, service learning projects, and other opportunities), it would have improved the students' chances of graduating from high school. Outside studies have noted that clarifying the links between schools and getting a job may convince more students to stay in school. (Bridgeland, DiIulio, & Morison, 2006)

Textbox 3.1

Students are looking for real and meaningful interactions with the world around them. Service learning gives students more reasons to show up, try, and stay in school. The authors of *The Silent Epidemic* shared these recommendations (see below) to decrease the rate of school dropouts in America, and service learning plays a key role in this process.

Recommendations:

1. Researchers should directly examine the relationship between service learning and dropout prevention.
2. The U.S. Department of Education and state departments of education should work to increase access to service learning for every student.
3. Every school district should have a service learning coordinator who helps teachers implement effective programs and who encourages students—especially those at risk of dropping out—to enroll in classes that include service learning.

To help keep students in school and headed toward a brighter, fuller future, these recommendations should be implemented nationwide.

CIVIC RESPONSIBILITY

Students who participate in service learning gain knowledge about the world around them and become motivated to change and improve it. They learn about laws, politics, environment, communities, nonprofits, different socioeconomic levels; it often changes their perspective on the world. Students who participate in service learning have increased feelings of civic responsibility and engagement. This is obviously what we want from our citizens and future voters.

One study of 4,057 students from 52 high schools in Chicago found that they "foster notable improvements in students' commitments to civic participation. Discussing civic and political issues with one's parents, extra-curricular activities other than sports, and living in a civically responsive neighborhood also appear to meaningfully support this goal" (Kahne & Sporte, 2007).

Another study found impressive increases in student levels of civic engagement and responsibility as a result of service learning:

> Kahne and Westheimer (2003) used surveys, observations, interviews, and student work to study 10 such programs. In one project, some students spent a semester investigating whether residents in their neighborhood wanted curbside recycling, and others helped develop a five-year plan for the fire and rescue department. All the students collected data from citizens and government agency staff and presented their findings to their county board of supervisors. The researchers found that, compared with a control group, participating students made significantly larger gains in developing such civic skills as vision and community engagement. (David, 2009)

Boston teacher Jeremy Greenfield knows this. He leads service learning projects that focus on justice in local communities and empower his students.

> Learning that justice is not simply a subject in a book, but a day-to-day, life or death matter, students investigate the current state of their own community. Touring a neighborhood initiative and conducting interviews, students begin to explain how justice is served or not served in the community. As local issues and topics arise, the project becomes student-inspired and student-driven. After reading about urban ecology and environmental justice, one student wants to know, "Is my community environmentally safe?" A study of urban poverty and gangs helps another understand why there are so many neighborhood gangs. The culminating Community Justice Career Fair brings information to several classes of peers. By planning and carrying out this event, students learn the intricacies and difficulties of planning community action.

Meeting professional community activists connects the classroom experience to careers and demonstrates that Bringing Justice Home [the project name] starts with informed citizens. (Greenfield, n.d.)

Jeremy's work might have lasting effects—his students may be more likely to vote, to volunteer, to be informed, and to be leaders in their own communities. As a teacher who uses service learning as well, this is not surprising at all. Students live and breathe this work—it engages them in ways they might not have ever been engaged before. These new thoughts, new actions, and new connections can yield more informed, active, and responsible future American citizens. And with the problems facing our society today, we definitely need that!

IMPROVEMENTS IN POSITIVE BEHAVIORS AND ATTITUDES

As an educator, it is clear that students involved in service learning have more positive behaviors and attitudes about school. But we don't have to rely on one teacher's anecdotal observations. Now there is data to support these improvements in students' behavior and attitudes. One study outlines recent studies and the results:

About a dozen studies have been conducted over the past three years that have shown the impact of service-learning on students' academic achievement. Two state level studies are of note: In Michigan, students that participated in Learn and Serve–funded programs were compared to matched groups of students who did not participate in service-learning (Billig & Klute, 2003).

Researchers compared the students on measures of school engagement and on their performance on the Michigan Educational Assessment Program (MEAP). The study had 1,988 student respondents, 1,437 of whom participated in service-learning. Results showed that service-learning students in grades 7-12 reported more cognitive engagement in English/language arts (e.g., paying more attention to schoolwork, putting forth effort) than nonparticipants. For students in grades 2-5, students who participated in service-learning reported greater levels of behavioral, affective, and cognitive engagement in school than their nonparticipating peers, showing statistically significant differences in the effort they expended, paying attention, completing homework on time, and sharing what they learned with others. The Michigan study also revealed that service-learning students in the fifth grade demonstrated significantly higher test scores on the state assessment than their nonparticipating peers in the areas of writing, total social studies, and three social studies strands: historical perspective, geographic perspective, and inquiry/decision-making. (Billig, 2002)

In an article on Edutopia, the findings that show the many benefits of service learning are highlighted, as well as words from a veteran teacher who started using service learning as a learning tool.

> Benefits of service learning: Kids who are excited about what they learn tend to dig more deeply and to expand their interest in learning to a wide array of subjects. They retain what they learn rather than forget it as soon as they disgorge it for a test. They make connections and apply their learning to other problems. They learn how to collaborate, and their social skills improve. They are more confident talking to groups of people, including adults. And, as a number of research reports suggest, project-based learning correlates positively with improved test scores, reduced absenteeism, and fewer disciplinary problems.
>
> "I've seen test scores of students rise because of the engagement in project-based learning," says Gwendolyn Faulkner, former technology coordinator at Harriet Tubman Elementary School, in Washington, DC. "I saw my students mainstream out of English as a Second Language into the mainstream classroom. I saw my mainstream students scoring three and four grades above their grade level on standardized tests. I'm a convert." (Curtis, 2001)

COMMUNITY CONNECTIONS

This chapter has reviewed some current data about the benefits of service learning. But there are many less quantifiable benefits for schools and the community.

Consider the importance of students developing relationships with people outside of the school community. By interviewing local experts, elders, or other community members, students develop relationships and see the opportunities for themselves in a new way. Students who feel noticed, known, and included in their communities can feel more valuable and important. These qualities are sure to develop more confidence and more social skills, and banish some of the isolation that adolescence can cause.

The community can also view the school and students in a different light. Consider a local business owner's change of perspective about teenagers when they are helping community elders, fundraising for a nonprofit, or cleaning up a local park. These relationships can break stereotypes and change the perspectives of community leaders about students and the schools. This, in turn, can lead to more support for school budgets, a decrease in crime, and more involvement from the community in schools in real and powerful ways.

This chapter only scratches the surface of how students can benefit from service learning. Clearly, we see improvement in students' achievement, GPA, attendance, and sense of civil engagement and responsibility, and better behavior and attitudes through service learning. The reasons for integrating this powerful learning tool into your teaching are numerous and clear. The next chapter will explore a recent case study on the benefits of service learning for middle-level students.

RESOURCES

A review of articles linking service learning (and other extended learning opportunities) and reduced dropout rates, www.expandinglearning.org/expandingminds/article/proven-solu-tion-dropout-prevention-expanded-learning-opportunities.

Learning in Deed, a PDF about service learning from the National Commission Service Learn-ing: http://ed253jcu.pbworks.com/f/LearningDeedServiceLearning_American+Schools.PDF.

Practical Experience, Improved Self-Esteem among Benefits of Service Learning, www.humankinetics.com/excerpts/excerpts/practical-experience-improved-self-esteem-among-benefits-of-service-learning.

Studies to support project-based learning: www.edutopia.org/project-based-learning-research.

What Research Says about Service Learning and Civic Participation, www.ascd.org/publications/educational_leadership/may09/vol66/num08/Service_Learning_and_Civic_Participation.aspx.

Chapter Four

The Doing Revolution

*Service Learning Meets the Needs
of Middle-Level Students*

We move what we are learning from our heads, to our hearts, through our hands. —Brene Brown

As teachers and parents of middle school students know, adolescents face many challenges and rapid changes that impact their social, cognitive, and physical realms all at once. Traditional learning environments for middle school students are often not the best fit for the developmental needs of middle school students. Research tells us that students transitioning from an elementary school to a middle school (or junior high) experience less engagement and decreased parental communication, and are more at risk of isolation and bullying (Goldenring & Rosen, 2004). The manner in which early adolescents are schooled may not be the best developmental match to help middle-level learners achieve both academic and personal success

The focus of this case study is to learn if service learning better meets the needs of middle-level students in terms of their personal growth, which in my study, included engagement and self-efficacy. The research question was: How did fifth grade students' participation in a service-learning program influence their personal development, including their engagement and self-efficacy? It was important to tell the stories of the students in a service-learning environment, featuring their voices. Often, student voice is overlooked in educational policy and decision making. There is also very little research about middle-level service learning, so this resource sought both to fill that gap and to explore the student experience in a particular service-learning environment.

WHY MIDDLE SCHOOL?

Middle school students face not only the challenges of adolescence and transitioning to a new school but also increased disengagement from learning, decreased achievement, and less parental communication as they transition to middle school (Eccles et al., 1993). Middle school is often the last best chance to engage students in their learning and for them to experience success before the all-important ninth-grade year. Completing ninth grade on time is linked to increased rates of graduating from high school (McCallumore & Sparapani, 2010). The stakes could not be higher for the need to engage and motivate middle school students in their own learning.

THE CASE: RIVERDALE MIDDLE SCHOOL

Bridgeport (a pseudonym) is a small town in a northeastern state. It has a population of 5,064 people and sits just off a major interstate. The town has several small businesses in the main street intersection including restaurants, a bookstore, and shops. The community consists primarily of working-class and middle-class citizens. Some higher-income households are also part of the community.

Bridgeport has a racial makeup of 97.80 percent white, 0.26 percent African American, 0.12 percent Native American, 0.65 percent Asian, 0.26 percent from other races, and 0.89 percent from two or more races. 0.67 percent of the population is Hispanic or Latino. 3.3 percent of families and 6.1 percent of the population live below the poverty line, including 7.0 percent of those under age 18 and 4.9 percent of those age 65 or over. 23.2 percent of Bridgeport residents have a high school degree, and 44.1 percent have graduated with a bachelor's degree.

Supervisory Union

This district, or supervisory union, serves students from five different, but nearby small, rural towns. It has three elementary schools. One elementary school is located within the town of Bridgeport and feeds the Riverdale Middle School. The other elementary schools, located within two small rural towns, send its students to a seventh- to twelfth-grade middle and high school. The district is spread out geographically over twenty miles.

Riverdale Middle School

Riverdale Middle School is located just outside a small town in a New England state. It is rurally located, bordered by a farm, a stream, and some houses. The school serves students in grades 5–8. It houses 283 students and follows a middle school model.

Teachers

At the time of this study, there were thirty-four teachers at Riverdale. Of those thirty-four, 100 percent were Caucasian. Seventy-nine percent of the staff was female. All teachers were certified by the state, with eight teachers certified at level 1 and twenty-six teachers certified at level 2.

Environment

The researcher visited Riverdale during the first semester in November 2015. The middle school was a welcoming and active place. Visitors needed to sign in and were greeted by a large slideshow of current school activities and initiatives. The principal stood outside the school each day to greet students as they came off the buses at 7:30 a.m.

Once inside, the hallways were lined with student work. Students have lockers and were often clustered around homerooms. It was active, but not chaotic. Daily announcements let kids know when to arrive at their first class and offered any updates before wishing students and teachers a good day.

Riverdale was a lively middle school. The kids seemed generally happy to be there, as did the staff. Many teachers stood outside of their classes, talking with students or other teachers between classes. The feeling of the school was vibrant and dynamic.

THE PARTICIPANTS

The population of participants for this research was fifth-grade students at a rural middle school, in a small town, in a northeastern state. Every fifth- and sixth-grade student participates in a service-learning and leadership project during a sustainability course in his or her fifth- and sixth-grade year. Twenty-one students were part of this study. Detailed observations, focused interviews, and other qualitative tools were used to narrate student experiences in this service-learning and leadership project. Three school staff members were also part of this case study.

Sustainability Program

The sustainability program started in 2013 after it was proposed to replace a home economics program. This core science teacher noted the passing of the home economics program and proposed a four-year sustainability program for the middle school in its place. There was a small home economics classroom, with a kitchen attached, and some outdoor space that could be utilized, as well, for this new program.

The teacher gained approval for the course as an applied academic course. This meant that it would be different from the core academic courses offered, which included literacy, science, math, and social studies. Applied academics included art, physical education, technology, foreign language learning, and music. All students cycled through all of the applied academic courses each year in five- and ten-week sessions. The teacher would have ten students in a class and would facilitate a service-based progression of coursework in sustainability. Topics, projects, and responsibilities would increase in a progression as students moved through the courses. Each year students would explore issues in sustainability based on their choice and interests and a set of activities designed by the teacher. The idea was that these courses would give an authentic experience to students and allow them to create projects that improve their school and communities. This program was very unique in that sustainability is not often taught as an applied academic subject, and that the approach—service and project-based learning—would be the guiding pedagogy.

STUDY THEMES

Several themes emerged in this study through an iterative case study process. The full dissertation details all of these findings (Farber, 2016d), and these are in the list below. In the next section, they are grouped into and discussed in terms of the scope of this book and what might be helpful to practitioners and educational leaders.

KEY FINDINGS

- Students are "doing" throughout the course and are engaged.
- Students are building competency.
- Students are constantly problem solving.
- Students show caring regularly during the program (for chickens, each other, the grounds, and the program).
- Every student has a personal connection with the teacher.
- The students describe the learning environment as fun and relaxed.
- Students show increased independence.
- Students describe pride and feeling good about their daily work.
- The students find joy and fun in their work and the program.
- The program has significant schoolwide impacts.
- There are very few student behavioral problems in the sustainability classes.

- The sustainability program is integrated, applied academics, and learning.
- Students are learning to follow through on commitments and responsibilities.
- This program can dramatically change a student's perception of learning.

Further Findings

- Teacher growth mindset and bravery
- Innovative teaching needs support and a community to sustain itself.
- STEM initiatives and the greater good

STUDENTS DOING: BUILDING COMPETENCY, PROBLEM-SOLVING SKILLS, AND INDEPENDENCE

Students in this program were busy doing hands-on work (what I call simply doing) most of the time in class. In the sustainability program, they had a job to do: they had to learn how to take care of all the living creatures and systems that support the school and decreasing its environmental impact. If they were not actually working with their hands, they were planning, organizing, or reflecting with their classmates about how to improve the sustainability program. Learning was active and social. When the students started the class, they were nervous and unsure. They quickly moved from that to experimenting and doing.

The teacher set the stage and the moral imperative for the work:

> It was the eighth graders who build the chicken coop. Here's how sustainability works—in this class you will do things to add to, build, make things to build the program. Do more, add more. The next group continues that work that you started. The eighth graders built the coop for the chickens and for you. For the next generation.

Instantly, the group knew the *doing* was up to them. They knew that if they didn't take care of the jobs, if they didn't problem solve, the chickens, the program, and the tradition would not continue, and the living creatures would suffer. In this way, the chicken coop was a microcosm of the concept of sustainability. Students knew that they had the power to improve the chicken coop environment, the pond, the worms, and the classroom space, both indoors and out. The teacher made the connection that their care, responsibility, and problem solving was the thing that will continue the program and lead to a more sustainable world beyond.

The researcher witnessed students constantly problem solving and growing competence and independence throughout the study. The students came in unsure, and moved quickly with their own motivation and direction toward independence and competence. They were constantly reflecting, changing course, and trying new things. Students expressed this growth in myriad ways, through their projects, in their daily jobs and chores, in interviews, and in interactions with each other and the teacher. The teacher did not tell students how or when to do things. She asked questions of them, and wondered aloud what could be done. Such as, "That door to the coop fell off again. What do you think we should do about that?" Then a student would volunteer to try to fix it.

One student reflected on her contributions:

> I am really proud of finding a way the chickens could be warm in the winter and working as a team with my class to figure out the solution to the pond. The pond was a big job. Since winter was coming, we had to drain the pond. We knew that, but how were we going to keep the expensive tarp underneath from freezing? Our class came up with an idea of putting a tarp over it. It was a big job because we had to remove all the rocks, and plants and, the hardest part of all, the fish. At the end, it was a success and everybody felt good about what they had accomplished.

Independence was built from the moment kids walked into class, in subtle and overt ways. Right by the door was a white board that listed all the sustainability jobs, which included taking the temperature, letting chickens out, refreshing water, filling the food dish, shoveling snow, collecting eggs, cleaning nesting boxes, freshening sawdust, managing food scraps, cleaning the kitchen and floors, emptying compost and recycling bins, and caring for the worm bin, pond, and garden tower. Students signed up at the beginning of class to complete a set of jobs. This first act was one of choice and independence. When they wrote their names down, students were committing to do the job. They were proclaiming their choice, independence, and competence. The teacher noticed that the job sign-up board became much more than she had anticipated:

> I think they really, really love that that idea of walking in, and knowing that they have 10–15 minutes to just sort of show what they can do. And, take that on and write their name on the board—it's so funny, that board—writing their name on that board is such a thing. And that was just my own mental, so I would remember what we had to do everyday. And that became something that I had no idea would be such a thing. And it's really an ownership thing, and um, having them like assign their name to something, and then walk away knowing that they can carry that through. I never saw the power in that.

The students developed independence and confidence in their ability to complete a job. The teacher had put her trust in these kids that they could do this work, and they showed her what they could do when they signed up to complete a job and follow through.

By giving students the chance to focus on active learning with a moral goal (reducing the environmental impact of the school), the students were able to grow their problem solving, competence, and independence over time. At a time when students developmentally crave active, social learning, with choices, this program seemed to match these needs. Students were invited into problem-solving and leadership roles, and took them. As a result, they were deeply engaged. Often these students would want to come in and continue the work during recess or other open times in their schedules—they were so motivated and engaged by this type of active learning.

LEARNING IS PERSONAL: JOY, PRIDE, CARE, AND CONNECTION

Connected deeply to this personal growth of students was the difference of the class in terms of joy, pride, care, and connection. The teacher created a joyful, lighthearted climate in several ways. She connected to each student personally. She knew students' families, knew their hobbies or extracurricular activities, and asked students about them. She went out of her way to connect with each student each day. She laughed easily and often with students. She also played music during her classes, which helped students relax and settle in for sustainability. This might seem minor, but it helped set the stage for deeply personal, positive, and engaged work.

Students in this class were asked to care. The teacher had said, "You will build something. You are handing down the service and the responsibility, handing it down and leaving things for the next generation." This created a culture of caring and responsibility in the students. They were the custodians and keepers of this program and the space. Students noted the importance of caring in their interviews and written work, and it emerged as a theme from the interview with the principal.

The school principal noticed the effects of the culture of caring in a boy that had trouble working with others. "I see this both directly and indirectly, like I have a young man my den (homeroom) who is an 8th grade boy, for who I was wondering for a long time does he have a caring gene in his body?—But when I see him out there with the chickens and he picks them up, now I see it." Sometimes it takes caring for other living things for caring to emerge in students. It is much harder to show caring and compassion for other early adolescents for some students. Caring for the chickens was a direct experience that these students had the responsibility for each day and it was practice for caring and compassion in other settings.

Another boy defined *sustainability* as "how to take care of stuff, take care of chickens, worms . . . and mostly taking care of things." The researcher asked him, "So how does it feel to take care of things? How does that feel to you?" He responded, "It feels better than just doing nothing."

The power of caring for other creatures was felt by all of the students the researcher observed. A group of students worked on a slideshow at the end of the class and said this about caring for the chickens:

> Our sustainability class loves the chickens! We love taking care of them, and we also love feeding them. But we especially love holding them! We love doing all the jobs, and we are really interested in everything we do in Sustainability so we love coming to sustainability every day.

On almost every questionnaire, the students identified taking care of the chickens as one of the things they were most looking forward to. In the interviews, taking care of the chickens was a constant theme. This experience of caring for other living things and for the class community has the potential to improve how these students care for others, animal and human, in the future. Linked with the idea of care was pride. Students showed that they were proud to have an impact on their school and community. They felt good about making a difference. Students at this age want to feel heard and important. This contribution helped them feel pride in their work and its impact.

LEARNING HAS AN IMPACT:
SCHOOL, COMMUNITY, BEHAVIOR

This pride came from the many things the students were able to accomplish in their sustainability course. Its impacts were wide reaching and easily seen by students and the community. They weren't just doing something for a test, or for one teacher. They were doing something beyond that, something that mattered to their school and community. Impacts included:

- running a composting program for the school, including teaching students how and why to compost at lunch.
- creating, running, and managing a chicken coop. This included collecting eggs, collecting data about the eggs, delivering them to the cafeteria to be used in the school lunch program. This also included feeding and caring for the chickens, including creating safe and comfortable nesting boxes, feeding and watering them, and making sure their environment was clean and safe.
- constructing and managing a small pond. This included preparing the area for winter, moving the fish, and covering it to prepare for the next season.
- designing an information campaign to share the impacts of bottled water on the environment. They petitioned the school board to remove the vending machines that contained bottled water and supplied each student (after

fundraising) with a metal water bottle featuring a student's design to use instead.
- creating artwork from unrecyclable bottle caps for the school's hallways.
- selling eggs and greens to the community to encourage local eating and to support continuing the program.
- This year, the students are hard at work on building a greenhouse. They hope to grow more local food to feed students in the school, to close the loop on food production, and to promote healthy living.
- There are more impacts, depending on the grade and focus of the curriculum for that year's sustainability class, but this gives you an idea of the kinds of impacts this program can have on a school.

Teachers often say they need a public relations (PR) department. No one knows the amazing things teachers do with students unless it is somehow shared. This program has so many school impacts that are clearly visible, so community members know about it and value the program. Students regularly give tours of the school and the sustainability program, extending its reach. This leads to more investment from the community, parents, and students.

In addition, because there is so much active learning (or doing) in these classes, there are significantly few behavior disruptions and problems. One teacher explained why she thought this was the case:

> So when we get students every year from the elementary school, they come up here. We always get a list of the students and I don't know them. And she sees all of these students and so I will go to her and say "Can you tell me a little about these kids that are coming up?" Um, and what I am looking for, you know, are how do they learn, you know, are there any that have behavioral difficulties that I should be aware of? And she will know those kids, but she will also point out that you have to have them, again, engaged and involved. She just doesn't see those (negative) behaviors in her program. Because the kids take ownership for what they are doing. And they are so proud of it. For everything, they have a role. They have a purpose each day when they go in there and so their presence in that class makes a difference in what they do.
>
> The researcher witnessed this as well. Students in this program were engaged and for the most part, focused. There were few if any disruptions. Students encouraged each other and participated in active learning, problem solving, and reflection.

This is a brief summary of the themes of this case study. For more information, please see the full dissertation. The bottom line is programs like this have a profound impact on students at the middle level. It seems to be a developmental fit for this age group, and can increase self-efficacy and engagement. What follows are the findings and recommendations based on this research.

KEY FINDINGS

- Middle-grade students need choice.
- Middle-grade students need to feel competency and gain skills with problem solving in a mistake-friendly setting.
- Middle-grade students need to feel connected personally to teachers, students, and authentic tasks for engagement to occur.
- Middle-grade students need to feel that they are making a difference and improving their schools and communities.

To meet developmental needs and engage middle-level students, these elements should be a central part of any middle-level education program. Creating environments by using project-based or service learning, coupled with efforts to connect personally to students, can meet these goals and truly engage and motivate middle-level learners.

EFFECTS ON ENGAGEMENT

- Students are engaged cognitively, emotionally, and behaviorally.
- Students feel school membership and do authentic work.
- Students feel good about being involved in something that they feel will make the world a better place.

Students in service and project-based learning environments by the very nature of the work are engaged cognitively, emotionally, and behaviorally. The daily work provides a vehicle for this type of authentic engagement. When tied to school identity and service, students feel connected to each other and to a cause greater than themselves. This provides students with meaning, purpose, and identity, at a time when these are shifting in terms of development.

RECOMMENDATIONS

- A sustainability or service-learning program in every middle school or school that teaches students grades 5–8.
- Consider K–8 configurations for more service opportunities and stage fit.
- Integrate service learning in existing programs.
- When starting new and innovative programs, provide a system for supporting the teacher and the program.
- Cultivate growth mindset on the part of all teachers and students.
- Create authentic learning experiences, projects, and activities for middle school students that connect them to the wider world.

Based on this case study research, the summary themes, and findings presented here, these recommendations are offered to middle-level educators, leaders, and policy makers. It is recommended that every middle school learning environment use service or project-based learning to promote engagement and personal development of students. Kindergarten through eighth-grade schools, if created with best practices for middle school design in mind, can create an environment where students can serve the school community as leaders. They also then do not have to transition to a new school when they are most developmentally at risk of decreasing engagement and parental communication, and at an increased risk of bullying and isolation.

Teachers are at risk of becoming islands of innovation, where there is little support or community around their service or project-based learning programs. These teachers need support with this complex and challenging work. Growth mindset is a key attribute of strong learning environments, for both teachers and students. Innovation, creativity, and moving out of comfort zones is hard work, and learning communities need the support to make mistakes in the learning and growing process. Lastly, projects for middle-level students must connect to the wider world; otherwise, it lacks relevance and connection for students.

This case study provided a window on early adolescent students' experience in a robust and challenging service-learning program. The students were engaged in this work and it provided them with self-efficacy and positive learning experiences that could affect their lives for years to come. As one student said about the impact of this kind of learning:

> I didn't like school. I didn't want to learn anything when I came here. Now, it is almost the end of the year, and I feel like it's only been a month. I think I have changed because I am actually wanting to learn. And most kids don't. Myself. My whole self. My whole personality changed from not wanting to learn to wanting to learn.

Isn't that what we want for all of our students? To want to learn and to feel important and valuable, and ready to solve our world's most complex problems?

RESOURCE

The Doing Revolution: Service Learning, Early Adolescents, and Personal Growth, unpublished doctoral dissertation by Katy Farber.

Chapter Five

Building a Service and Project-Based Learning Climate

I alone cannot change the world, but I can cast a stone across the waters to create many ripples. —Mother Teresa

Teachers can have big dreams of creative, innovative projects and engaged students in their classrooms. We want to see students who are busy researching, collaborating, creating, and solving authentic problems they are interested in. But this doesn't happen without a strong community of learners, in a safe, respectful, and supportive learning environment. This must be built intentionally.

WHY BUILD A STRONG CLASSROOM COMMUNITY?

Service and project-based learning is a great way to engage students in their own learning. But if the community doesn't feel safe to take risks and be supportive, it can fall flat. The personalized, deep kind of authentic learning that takes place in service learning and project-based learning classrooms is dynamic, responsive, and focused on a growth mindset. Student must feel that they can safely explore challenging topics in a collaborative environment. Here are some ways to build a strong, supportive, and inclusive community that is ready to engage and be inspired by relevant, meaningful projects.

TEAM-BUILDING ACTIVITIES

During the planning for the first few weeks of school, it is important to build trust, community, and shared experiences. One way to do this is to schedule regular team-building activities. These are a fun break from hearing about expectations and instead doing get-to-know-you activities because they are often physical and challenge different learning styles. Work with your team to schedule some longer blocks of time during the first month of school. It is also helpful (and sometimes critical) that these have more supervision. Team-building activities work well with groups of eight to ten students for more involved challenges, so ask your physical education teacher or guidance counselor to help you organize and facilitate this time. There are many great team-building books and online resources available, and some are listed at the end of this chapter.

OWNERSHIP OF THE SPACE

Picture this: all of the desks grouped and organized, with materials where they should be, and everything is neat and orderly. Many teachers love to set up their classrooms just the way they think their students would like it. But someone is left out of the equation here: the student! "Giving students their choice of work space empowers them to make their own decisions and monitor their own behavior" (Solarz, 2015).

To build student voice, consider how you can use your classroom's physical space to give students choice and help them feel comfortable. Just think about how kids love having ownership of their own rooms. Many create little nooks and spaces with more detail and creativity than we could imagine. Kids want to create spaces at home and in the classroom that allow them room to be flexible, to be inspired, and to collaborate.

At the beginning of the year or semester, set up a "rough draft" of the classroom, and ask for student feedback and ideas. Often the best ideas come from students, and they will feel empowered about designing learning spaces that fit their needs. Students can give feedback about desk spacing, reading areas, independent work areas, decorations, and collaboration spaces. They need to make the space feel like their own. Some students are coming from homes where they cannot do this, so this simple act can help some students feel more comfortable in your class. It also sets the tone for honoring different learning styles. Some students need to sit by the door. Some need more room to spread out. Others need a quiet, organized space free of distractions. And yet others want to work on the floor, or on a bean bag. By creating flexible classrooms and space, you are honoring these differences with your actions.

DEVELOP COMMUNITY NORMS

Students need to know what to expect to feel safe in a classroom. What is expected? If you are a Responsive Classroom school, this is nothing new, but it is vital. Middle school philosophies and pedagogies, like advisories, also encourage the setting of norms in any class or student group.

Help your class design a set of norms (sometimes called rules) that guide everyone. They usually boil down to respecting yourself and others, but student voice and wording matter here. It should come from them. Ask students: "How would you like our class to feel? What will help you learn the very best and be inspiring and motivating to you?" Then list all the ideas in a brainstorm. Wait a day or two if possible; then whittle these down to a few guiding principles. Print out a large version for students to sign and then you can hang it in the meeting area. Share a copy with parents, too, so they know the expectations for the class. This is something that you can refer to often during the year. Students will need reminders about how to work in a caring, strong community. You can refer back to the norms and have students reflect on them by saying, "Please review our class norms and see which one you might want to work on today," or as a class, "How have we been doing with our class norms? Which ones do we want to focus on and improve?" Then any reminders become less personal, and more just following up on the group's established norms.

MODEL COMMUNITY DISCUSSIONS

Students are interested in the world happening around them. What was mom listening to on the radio? What is happening with my friend's family? Why does my teacher seem worried about the big test coming up? Students need safe communities to discuss events happening in their classrooms, schools, and communities. Otherwise, they will get the information somewhere else, and it may be riddled with inaccuracies, stereotypes, and biases.

During the first few weeks of school, it is critical that students learn how the class will solve problems, work out difficult issues, and discuss complex events (in the world or in literature). Brainstorm with the class what makes a good discussion on chart paper. List out the characteristics of what students agree makes a good discussion. Then have a few students do a "fishbowl," where they make a smaller circle within a larger one. The small circle should discuss an issue, such as some current event or a book they have read. The outer circle watches and notes how it went. Discuss and show what it looks like to encourage someone to speak who has not participated yet ("What do you think, Sarah?"). Show and describe what it is like to disagree respectfully ("I have a different opinion about this, and here is why . . ."). Share ideas and create norms for small- and large-group discussions. Ask the students to ponder:

Is everyone heard? Did we disagree but show respect?
Did we supply evidence to support our ideas?

Modeling goes a long way, especially since in the media there are lots of examples of the opposite.

DEVELOP STRONG RELATIONSHIPS

Students want to be seen and feel heard. They want to feel welcome, positive, and a part of something. Use the first few weeks of school to try to connect to each student. Schedule activities that let you get to know students personally. Pay attention to what students share and then ask follow-up questions. What sports do they play? What are their hobbies? Who are their friends? Listen. Be excited to see them. This is the foundation of a strong class community.

GROWTH MINDSET

This one is so important and often overlooked by our culture and in building classroom communities. Students need to know that the classroom and community is a safe place for making mistakes. They need to know they won't be embarrassed by either the students or teachers for stretching, trying something new, taking chances with their learning. Students need to feel okay about trying out new ideas, changing their minds, and disagreeing. The way the teacher speaks and encourages this creates an environment where this is the norm.

Taking this one step further, students need to know that mistakes grow their brains, and that they are helpful in the learning process. In the resources section there is a great website all about growth mindset in math, and growth mindset activities and visuals. Make a chart that lives in the classroom about growth mindset and refer to it often. Consider retooling your own language to support a growth mindset—by encouraging things like the YET rule. In my classroom, we had "YET" written in large letters on a large student-made poster. When students expressed frustration about not being able to do something, we added *YET* to the statement, such as "I can't do fractions, YET." This encouraged progress and possibility.

BUILD STUDENT LEADERSHIP

Students will be more engaged and motivated if they have leadership roles in class from day 1. The goal is to build a functioning student-led learning environment where the students themselves are leading and running the classroom. Here are a few ideas for how to build leadership opportunities in the class, with inspiration from the helpful book *Learn Like a Pirate*, by Paul Solarz (2015), and posted about at the Tarrant Institute for Innovative Education blog (Farber, 2016c).

> *Give me 5:* Students and teachers can interrupt classes at any time for announcements, "ah-ha" moments, or questions, or to share resources. All students have this power. It needs to be taught and modeled. See this post for more on Give me 5 and other ideas to promote students' leadership.
>
> *Student jobs in the classroom:* Students are responsible for tasks that build community and responsibility (tech maintenance, writing homework on class blog or whiteboard, reviewing the day before, catch up students who were absent).
>
> *Build community by pairing kids in different groups for activities:* You can use popsicle sticks to randomize this so partners are always changing.
>
> *Responsibility partners:* For larger projects, assign a responsibility partner to students. This student can help brainstorm ideas, and they can keep each other on task and problem solve.
>
> *Reflection and responsibility for learning:* Move students toward shared responsibility for learning. Ask these at the end of the period or day: "What can I do better next time? How can I help my peers do better?" This promotes collective responsibility and individual leadership. All boats sink or rise together.

The beginning of the school year is a zany time for teachers and students both. There is so much to do. When you build a strong classroom community, students learn they are part of an inclusive, responsive, and respectful learning community and can challenge themselves to do high-quality, relevant, and exciting project-based learning.

RESOURCES

Get to know students personally. Ice breaker activities: www.educationworld.com/a_lesson/lesson/icebreakers_for_kids_2.shtml.

Growth mindset ideas: www.pinterest.com/explore/growth-mindset-activities.

A helpful handbook for building student leadership and voice: *Learn Like a Pirate,* by Paul Solarz.

A program for building class community, student voice, and choice: Responsive Classroom: www.responsiveclassroom.org.

Chapter Six

Gathering Ideas

Good ideas are common—what is uncommon is people who will work hard enough to bring them about. —Buddha

What teacher doesn't love the energy and excitement generated when you brainstorm a list of ideas? Students are creative, divergent thinkers who never cease to amaze me with their unique perspectives and ideas. That said, it can be a challenge to help students brainstorm within a particular curricular area, and then focus these creative ideas into actual realistic questions and topics for service learning. This chapter will help you guide your students from wild idea to focused topic, in a way that honors student choice and interest, as well as positive grouping and curricular goals.

DISCOVERING YOUR TOPIC AND CURRICULAR NEEDS

Before you can brainstorm with students, you need to decide what curricular areas you plan on addressing within your district or school's curriculum. For elementary teachers who teach all academic content areas, decide which subject or subjects you would like to complete a project in (literacy, math, social studies, or science). For middle school and high school teachers, within your content area, consider what unit or theme you would like the project to be a part of. Consult your district curriculum or the Grade Level Expectations, the Common Core State Standards, the Next Generation Science Standards, or other standards your school is focused on for standards that need to be addressed, within an academic subject, or as an integrated unit. Service learning does not stick to one content area, so students will explore different academic and real-world subjects as the project progresses, but you can have specific learning goals or standards in mind when you begin.

To see a list of possible project ideas by content area, see appendix 6.1.

Try to identify between six and ten standards, proficiencies, learning targets, objectives or curricular goals before you begin the project. These are concepts you need students to understand by the end of the project, and are expressly linked to (or even quoted from) your school's curriculum, or state and national standards. Once you have this list, you can inform parents of these curricular goals before you begin (see appendix 6.1).

When you have these curricular goals outlined, you can either plan lessons to meet these before you begin the project, as prerequisite knowledge, or you can tailor the project to include these concepts. If you choose to have students meet the curricular goals with the project itself, write a series of focused questions that can guide your students. These questions should be open ended, using higher-level thinking skills from Bloom's taxonomy (see appendix 6.2) to guide students into deep critical thinking about a topic.

After you've written a few questions, target the specific areas you would like to focus on. Then include these key components throughout the project, in student assessments, project requirements, and reflections. The more you address these curricular goals, the more likely students will meet and exceed your expectations. In some of my projects, I've kept the questions very open ended, and followed student interest freely. In others, I focused more on three to four concepts. Think about your curricular needs and goals, as well as your philosophy about student learning, as you design these questions.

In appendix 6.3, you'll find an example of the guiding questions that I wrote to inspire and motivate students to reflect on what they want to learn and the learning goals I wanted them to achieve. Your guiding questions will be vastly different depending on your topic area. You can also have students list topics instead of questions. The resulting ideas and projects met standards (and went way beyond) in the curricular areas and standards I selected.

THE GUIDING QUESTION BRAINSTORM

Now you've got your curricular goals and your guiding questions. What next? It's time to bring in the students. Give each student your guiding questions, and give them ample time to brainstorm and answer them fully. They should be able to do it independently, in teams, or in small groups. The idea is to have the room buzzing with ideas and excitement about the idea of studying what they want to! This is a liberating and empowering idea that will excite many students.

Students who have been in a more traditional learning environment might need prompting to expand their minds and think creatively. Encourage students to write down all of their ideas without limitation. This is an idea-generating time free from judgment. You can also set out items to help students along in their thinking, such as maps, historical artifacts, field guides, photos, anything that has to do with your topic that might spark some creative thinking. You might also lead this brainstorming activity as a whole class on a SMART or whiteboard.

Once you've collected the responses (or can look back at the SMART or whiteboard), and you have some time, sit down on your own and begin listing the consistent themes and topics you see. List all of these, grouping similar ideas into phrases or questions on a master list (see appendix 6.4). You will probably have at least twenty or so topic areas. Type these up, and then get ready to help the students prioritize their interests. You could also do this live on a SMART board, or on a brainstorming technology tool like Padlet.

Copy your new student-generated question list for each student. During the next class period, explain that students should number the questions in order of preference from one to five. Giving five different choices will give you some room for grouping needs and issues. It is essential that students' choices reflect their personal interests, not their friends'. For that reason, it should be a silent, independent activity. Also, students should know that the teacher will seriously consider their preferences, along with many other considerations, such as group dynamics, student abilities, and concerns.

THE CRUCIAL TASK: DEVELOPING SERVICE LEARNING TEAMS

Now this task will take some time. Try to set aside a planning period for a thoughtful reflection of student groupings. There are many issues to consider while creating service-learning teams.

First, take a look overall at the students' selections to get a sense of patterns and popular ideas. Then list out several group titles you feel will be represented (it helps to do this all in pencil, as it can change frequently). This is not set in stone, and as you sort through student responses you can add or change the teams as needed.

Next, go through the student responses, penciling students into different groups, considering student ability, gender, special needs, and group dynamics. Teams can range from two to four people, a size I've found optimal for service-learning projects. Any more than that and the teamwork seems to break down, especially with upper-elementary and middle school students.

Continue to group students this way, working from the list, and what you know about each child. It is important not to rush this, because often the success of the project is really based on the members of the group and how they work together. If you work in a team of teachers, or you are a new teacher, it would be helpful to ask your colleagues to take a look at your draft of groupings for any ideas or concerns. It is also helpful to touch base with the special educator in your school for feedback about specific student needs in teams.

Textbox 6.1
Gathering Ideas Summary

1. Teacher selects subject area and curricular goals.
2. Teacher creates a few guiding questions for students in a subject area, with the curricular goals in mind.
3. Students answer the guiding questions, coming up with their own questions about a topic (this can be done on paper individually or on a smart/whiteboard as a class).
4. Teacher collects the student responses and organizes them into project topics (or titles).
5. Teacher starts assigning students to particular topics based on interest, student ability, gender.

HELPFUL GROUPING HINTS

- When you group students of different abilities, don't always put one high-achieving student to lead the group. It isn't fair that our high-achieving students are always put in this role. Instead, think about pairing students with a similar ability level, or having two students at about the same level and two students at a different level within a group.
- Carefully look at behavioral needs. This is a project with some freedom and independence, and students who are likely to get each other off-task should not be together.
- Students with special needs can participate in regular groups but might need specific tasks and supports to help achieve group goals.
- Consider the classroom support you may have. Classroom assistants, parent volunteers, and administrators might be available at different times to support teams. With this kind of learning, all school staff are teachers!

Once your teams are ready, your students are close to beginning their service-learning experience! Now it is time to plan for the project using your class schedule, school schedule, and the unit's duration. In chapter 7, "Planning Considerations, Step by Step," we'll look at how to plan the whole experience, because timing is crucial to the project's success.

In the appendices for this chapter (6.1–6.5) are examples from an integrated unit in science and social studies, but they can be adapted to any subject.

RESOURCES

Brainstorming technology tools: www.techlearning.com/default.aspx?tabid=100&entryid=8315.

Brainstorming methods for the classroom: https://k12teacherstaffdevelopment.com/tlb/how-can-i-facilitate-brainstorming-in-the-classroom.

How to Develop Service Projects: www.learning-for-life.org/exploring/resources/99-720/y05.pdf.

Chapter Seven

Planning Considerations, Step by Step

To accomplish great things, we must not only act, but also dream; not only plan, but also believe. —Anatole France

Teachers will find that by doing some planning in advance, service-learning projects can be much more enjoyable for teachers (and students). By considering the ideas in this chapter before you begin creating, organizing, and assessing service-learning projects, you can be more comfortable and relaxed throughout the experience (and believe me, I learned this the hard way!). It is beneficial if you do these planning steps either before the student brainstorming outlined in chapter 6 ("Gathering Ideas"), or simultaneously. This will give your team teachers a chance to join you in this work.

SCHEDULES AND TIMING

The first thing you'll need to decide is the unit length and time period. Most projects take at least four weeks, working at least one hour per day. This is a very general guideline for upper-elementary and middle-grade students. More time would likely be beneficial for younger students.

Some schools do service learning as an integrated unit, working for two or more hours a day, for several weeks. This format does allow for more depth in the project, and potential off-site work.

And in some cases, integrated service-learning projects take all day, with all teachers from all academic subjects assisting and encouraging students to reach out beyond one particular academic area. These are often designed as a staff, and goals are embedded throughout the project in multiple disciplines. For example, a month-long middle school integrated unit on the environment includes specific content learning, guided by student interest and curricular goals; then students develop lesson plans to teach to the elementary schools about this topic. Students can then travel in teams to the various elementary schools and teach these lessons as a service to the community.

Another way to handle the timing of the project is to work backward from the culminating event. Select the most appropriate date for the final event, discussing it with your school's administrative assistant and consulting the school calendar to ensure there are no conflicts. Count backward at least four weeks from that date to determine when to begin the project.

TEAM WITH YOUR PEOPLE
(THE TEACHER TEAM AND THE PRINCIPAL)

Now that you have your timing worked out, it's time to bring in your team-mates. During your weekly unit meeting (hopefully you have one—if not, schedule a working lunch or meet during a prep period), share the timing for your project with your team teachers. Look for ways you can work together and support the learning in each other's classrooms. If your team teacher is working with you on the project, share the responsibilities such as the other items on this list, or those suggested in the next chapter, partnering with the community. Also, your team teachers can help you troubleshoot issues that might not have occurred to you in your planning. It will also help to have them on board because you will ultimately need their support and flexibility (not to mention any random materials a student group might need!).

Meet with your special education team. Share the curricular goals, schedule, dates, and any assessments you've developed. With service learning, you will get the highest buy-in from all students, special education or not. They will be motivated and want to contribute. So it is crucial that the special education team meet to identify students that might need extra support and come up with ways to accommodate the assessment and project, if needed. Any paraprofessionals can be assigned to assist groups with lower-functioning students to ensure stronger teamwork and support.

With service learning, students are often researching, guided by interest and the topic. Special education students will need support with this level of research and writing. There are ways everyone can be included in service-learning projects. As a team, students work out a timeline and delegate responsibilities. The special education team can brainstorm specific tasks and responsibilities for students needing lots of educational support and guidance. Meeting with your special education team will help you get out in front of any issues that might arise and plan to meet the needs of special education students in a student-led and -driven project such as this.

Once you have unit duration, a date for the culminating event, and a date of assessment and projects due, meet with the principal (or principals) to discuss how he or she can be supportive. You will potentially need funding, volunteers, good press to parents and school boards, and general goodwill for the project. The more organized you can be before this meeting, the better. If you have to, you can point to the measurable amounts of student improvement on standardized test scores for students (see chapter 3 and the talking points in appendix 2.1) who participate in service learning. And you can point out the data that shows service learning improves graduation rates, civic responsibility, motivation, and school attendance just to seal the deal. Often, schools have discretionary funds in small amounts that principals control. You might want to explain that as the project proceeds, unforeseen expenses might come up (think: seeds, plants, poster board, sign-making materials, recycling bins), and see if you might be able to access alternative funds. If not, there are more ways to secure funding that will be discussed in chapter 12, but this is definitely an area to explore with your principal.

Go out of your way to talk with the custodians, school cook, librarian, and technology support people about your project. They will be instrumental to your success with these projects. Why? On any given day during the project you might need to send students to these people to ask questions, do research, get materials, or learn a skill. They will need to be invested and aware of the project so they know students might be coming their way. Also, they might need ideas for how to guide them. Early one-on-one chats with these people (particularly the ones you think will be impacted most—such as projects on local eating might impact the school cook more than the custodian, but planting a garden impacts the school custodian and/or groundskeeper more) can smooth over any potential conflicts and provide more buy-in and support from these parties.

Take a few minutes at a staff meeting to explain what you are doing. At the staff meeting, briefly explain to staff (and support staff) what service learning is, what the focus of this year's project is, what they might see, and how they might be helpful. Then send out an email with the same information. This will head off any potential misunderstandings when students are using the phone to call experts, looking for the custodian for a shovel to begin their herb garden, or congregating outside in a habitat.

In some schools, special passes will be needed, or a procedure for student teams to gain access to resources and space for their work. Adult supervision will be needed for specific projects, and this will need to be worked out in advance (paraprofessionals, parent volunteers, and specials teachers are all good for this role). This will not look like traditional education. Students will be empowered and getting their hands dirty, literally in some cases and figuratively in all cases. This is not easy or quick work.

School staff may notice more freedom and liberty with this project, and they might need some help to understand and support it. Also, by explaining this to all school staff, you see who might be a good resource for your students for assistance such as materials, support, expertise, guidance, media support, and small-group supervisors. Many school staff will be excited about this project, some will be too busy to care much about it, and some will think it is not education at all. This will vary from school to school. As the school staff sees the engagement, success, and excitement the projects bring to the school, their ideas about this kind of learning will grow as well.

PLAN THE ASSESSMENT AND NEEDED RESOURCES

Now that you have some dates and a schedule, and support from your fellow teachers and building leader, start planning for the main assessment of the project. A portfolio system is discussed (and reproducible materials are in appendix 10.1) for this in chapter 10. Use this, or develop your own assessment, featuring the curricular goals you outlined in the last chapter. Rubrics often work well for this. You could use a combination of a portfolio and a project rubric.

Consider that in the culminating event, you want students to feature their work through visual, written, and oral forms. By using these three modalities, students can showcase their work in a way that is meaningful to them and have a greater impact because their message will be learned more fully if presented in several different ways. For example, students preserving an amphibian habitat on their school property might perform a skit about the species that live there, show the signage they created to protect the area, and present the group with an amphibian guide to the school campus. In that way, they are sharing their knowledge in a written, visual, and oral way for a greater impact. The assessment can reflect these different modalities.

Next, you'll want to brainstorm or locate any potential resources you may need for the project. This might involve help from the community, which will be outlined in the next chapter. But start listing your needs now, so you can begin to anticipate areas where you need support, funding, or volunteer donations. That way when the opportunity arises to fulfill a need, you will be ready.

ORGANIZE YOURSELF

If you are anything like many teachers, you have "to do" lists all over your desk, and other notes scrawled on Post-its. With service learning (as most of teaching), the amount of material and paperwork to manage can be overwhelming unless you have a system in place.

Teachers are unique in their systems for organization, but here are a few ideas:

- Set up a binder (or online folder) with all your service-learning plans, brainstorms, schedules, assessments, and contact information. Accordion folders also work well for managing larger amounts, as do Padlet or online organizers.
- You may want to have a folder or section of a binder for each student group. That way you can keep resources, observations, and assessments separate. They are also very easy to find this way. You can also use Google Docs to keep and collaborate on running records of groups.
- Have a file on your computer or server devoted to a year's or semester's service-learning projects. Save all materials in that folder, and hopefully you can find it and use it again next year. This is also a great way to save project examples from one year to the next.
- Save hard copies of everything—assessments, project work, observations, photos, all of it—so you can have a valuable service-learning resource in years to come. This is particularly handy if a computer or server crashes—you still have evidence of your projects. This is also an impressive project to add to your teaching portfolio.

PLAN FOR THE CULMINATING EVENT

The big show is important. After all your students' hard work, you really want to showcase their great work to parents and the whole school community. Thinking out a plan in advance will help you see where you are going and ensure that nothing surprises you (well, not really—this is service learning after all, and it is always surprising!).

Briefly outline a plan for the culminating event. Will it be outside or inside? In what location would you like to have it? Consider how many people you will be inviting (the whole school, a grade, specific grades or groups) and who will actually come (probably about half of that number). Who do you have to ask and schedule with? If it is to be in the school cafeteria, you'll need to work with custodial and kitchen staff (that's why you had the one-on-one chat earlier!). If it is outside, you might need to coordinate with physical education or other scheduled outdoor activities. Will you need extra tables, chairs, or other materials?

Then, make a list and tuck it away for the days right before the culminating event. Also, make a list of what has to be done in the week and days before the event, such as inviting and scheduling visits from other classes (these usually need to be circulated at least one week in advance). It is good to do this via email with classroom teachers, about one to two weeks in advance. Then teachers can look at their schedules and plan when is best to visit with their students.

In the week before the event, call your local newspaper to describe the event and ask for a photographer, or email a press release (the good press will help support you, your school, and service learning—more on this in the next chapter). Be sure to invite parents in multiple ways: via the all school newsletter, your classroom newsletter or a class letter, and school website. Parents often need at least a week to change their work schedules to attend these during the school-day events.

This is what the culminating event might look like: a whiteboard shares the name of the service learning fair, such as "The Wonders of the Worcester Watershed!," and gives directions for visitors as to where the students and the projects are located. Students are in their teams, sitting together at stations outside of the school, or in the gymnasium. Their projects are set up on desks, and they have created a presentation about their projects for their particular audience. The school community that was invited visits these student stations for three to ten minutes each. In small groups, the visitors travel around each student team's station to hear all about the amazing service-learning projects the students completed. During this learning fair, the principal wanders to stations too, as well as any important community members, the superintendent, invited press, and parents.

PLAN FOR PRETEACHING

Students will likely need some background in the area of focus for the service-learning project. Say you are about to embark on service-learning projects about our current food system. You will need to preteach about the industrial food process currently used in the United States and worldwide, and the growing local and organic food movement. You might want to teach about the global climate change effects of shipping food worldwide, about the ecological effects (and history) of pesticide use, genetically modified food, and other ideas. You might want to have students discover these concepts on their own throughout the project, and plan for this, or you might want them to go into more depth with this prior knowledge.

What has worked for me was to teach the basics of the area of focus, such as ecology, government, journalism, or any topic. Then, use those concepts as a springboard for the project. For your particular level, you might want to do more or less preteaching. It is variable based on student age, topic, and curricular goals.

Like anything, service learning is improved (and is much more manageable for everyone) with a little planning in these different areas. Take notes as you proceed through your projects or write all over this section of the book, because the considerations you face at your school could be different and more extensive. This ongoing reflection will help you develop your skills as a service learning facilitator. Next, we'll look at how to partner with the community for successful service-learning projects.

RESOURCES

Project-based learning planning forms from Buck Institute for Education: www.bie.org/objects/cat/planning_forms.

Service Learning Teacher Planning Sheet: www.tolerance.org/supplement/multicultural-service-learning-teacher-planning-sheet.

Service Learning: A Guide to Planning, Implementing, and Assessing Student Projects, by Sally Berman.

Project-based learning planning resources from Edutopia: www.edutopia.org/blogs/tag/pbl-planning.

Chapter Eight

Partnering with the Community

Never doubt that a small group of thoughtful, committed citizens can change the world. Indeed, it's the only thing that ever has. —Margaret Mead

If the quote "It takes a village to raise a child" is true, then the same can be said of service-learning projects. It takes a team of caring, motivated adults to successfully lead a comprehensive service-learning project. Usually, teachers are the self-sufficient type, who can handle most classroom challenges, projects, and issues on their own. This is not one of those times. In fact, our society and world are shifting to a place of constant collaboration, reflection, and teaming up to solve the world's most vexing problems and issues. Shouldn't education be the same?

The more community involvement there is in service-learning projects, the more engagement, investment, and empowerment is given to both the students and the community members. Students need all kinds of role models, and service learning can allow students access to people they might never have met before. It is thrilling for students to see people in the community caring about what they are doing and what they have to say. It is also powerful for upper-elementary, middle, and high school students to explore differing roles and careers in the community.

It can seem daunting, especially to a new teacher, to figure out how to find community members and volunteers to help out with the project. What follows are clear strategies with examples for how to find, organize, and use volunteers from the community in your service-learning project. Using parental support in a positive way and gaining administrative support will be reviewed as well. Finally, we'll explore how to contact local media to promote your school's service-learning project so the community can celebrate all of your students' (and your!) hard work.

FINDING A COMMUNITY SAGE AND LOCAL EXPERTS

If you live somewhere far away from your school, or have limited knowledge about the community in which your school is located, it will be essential that you find a well-connected "community sage." This person ideally will have lived in the community for a long time. It could be the custodian, a fellow teacher or staff member, or maybe a parent of a current or former student. You will need to ask around, talk to people in the teachers' room, and search for information about community resources on the service-learning project's main topics. You could also email your school staff to see if anyone has any resources or information about your class's topics.

When you hear back from people or you find your "sage," start a contact log. This log will list all of the possible people you could contact (or better yet, students could contact) to help out. If your topic is environmental sustainability, for example, you'll want to write down the name and contact information for the Solid Waste Management district office in your area, the nearest recycling center, and any community organizations that have goals of lessening landfill waste. If your community contact knows individuals who are experts in this area, get their contact information. You personally won't be contacting these people, unless you want some background information, or you want to set up a field trip. It will be the students' responsibility to contact each person or organization, with support, as this is an important part of the learning experience. See appendix 8.1, which has a contact log for you and your students to use.

If you cannot find a "community sage" or need more experts, consider sending home a survey for the parents. At the beginning of the year, I send home a survey of parents about their hobbies, areas of interest, and the possibility of classroom volunteering (see appendix 8.2). Then, when I am beginning these projects, I pull them out and see who I could have my students contact if they need it. At the same time, you could ask parents if they are interested in volunteering with any other parts of the project. Who knows, you could have a business executive whose hobby is creating maps, birding, or gardening. Parents are a wealth of information that should be utilized in creating a rich educational experience for students.

PARENT SUPPORT: WHAT IT MIGHT LOOK LIKE, WHAT YOU MIGHT NEED

We all know that parents' ability to help within the classroom varies widely. The last thing you want is a parent you need to constantly direct, as that might take away time from your involvement with students, yet it is almost impossible to complete these projects without considerable support from parents or school staff.

It is critical that parents or school staff have a known, clear support role. Here are a few ideas that have worked well within my classroom:

- Field trip supervisor (or small-group supervisor): With approval from your administrator, a parent may be able to take a small group to meet with a local expert or to visit a business or organization that can help with their project. Students should have questions, clipboards, and pencils ready. This is a great support that allows you to be in the classroom with the other groups. Or this person could supervise a small group when an expert visits on site (which might be a safer bet in larger schools with more liability issues).
- Materials organizer: A parent might be able to help track down needed materials, such as water test kits, shovels, fish tanks, whatever it is!
- Photographer: A parent could document each group's work. This could then be used to help assess students, to promote the project, and to document the learning experience.
- Media contact: A parent could contact the local media so the community is informed about the project and has an opportunity to be a part of the celebration at the end of the unit. Emailing and calling local radio stations, newspapers, and television stations is difficult during a busy teaching day. This is a great way for parents to support service learning and generate positive press for the school.

As you plan for parental involvement, try to give clear roles and expectations so the experience will be successful for everyone involved.

ADMINISTRATIVE SUPPORT

Partnering with your principal as you begin a service-learning project will be extremely helpful. This is important because you will potentially need approval and support for any projects that are building- and campus-wide.

If the principal is new or has no experience with service learning, share some resources (like this book!) with him or her so they can more fully understand the benefits and process of service learning. As soon as you can, schedule a meeting with your principal before you begin a service-learning project (as discussed in the previous chapter). Provide an overview of the project, list any needed materials and resources, and explain how you see your principal being involved. In most cases, the principal gives approval and guidance about different school projects that will be created by your students.

For example, some of my students wanted to label a wetland area near our playground with signs to protect it from damage. They had to seek approval from the principal, the recreation department, and the custodian. Having an open-door policy also helps with principal communication. Ask your principal to stop by during class when students will be working on the project. This way, the principal will see service learning in action, and he or she will be able to provide leadership and support as needed.

We all know that principals can be insanely busy, so in reality your principal might not stop by at all. In that case, be sure to invite him or her to your culminating celebration. This will do several good things: it will hopefully impress your principal, who will then sing your praises to the community, it will build positive relationships with your students and the principal, and it will educate your principal about service learning in general.

GOOD PR: THE MEDIA!

One thing I've found very true in teaching: no one knows about all the great work you are doing with students unless you tell them. Many teachers don't want to toot their own horn, or seem too full of themselves. The truth is, if you don't publicize your great work in service learning, no one will know you are doing it. More importantly, community involvement is essential to a good project. It is also very helpful for your reputation and career!

You might have several students who need added challenges, and are not overwhelmed with the project. These students can be on the public relations (PR) team, and, with your support, they can help with the items listed below. This is a great way to motivate your students who love to write and talk with people.

Of course, we are trained teachers, and not PR executives. Here are some simple tips to generate media coverage of your project.

- Email or call your local paper, and describe the project, or send them a press release (see examples in appendixes 8.3 and 8.4). Share how many students are working on it, what exactly they are doing, what the impact will be, and how the projects will change the world. Newspapers love stories like this. Hopefully they will send out a reporter and photographer to meet with you and your students.
- Email or call the calendar coordinator at your local paper, and share with them the date of the community project celebration. This will be great exposure and increase student motivation.
- Call your local community radio station and have them list the community project celebration in their calendar. They might also be interested in

interviewing a student on the air. Use one of the members of your student PR team.

- Email the school staff to schedule visits to your students' stations during the community share. Set up a schedule for visits and put it in the teachers' room or do it online. Encourage the whole school to come out and view your students' amazing work.
- Send home an invitation to parents about the community celebration including date, time, length, and location. Also include this in your regular classroom newsletters, and on the school website.
- Make sure all the community volunteers are invited as well. Having the students who benefited from their expertise call them directly is a meaningful way for these volunteers to be included.
- Have your students make posters about the community celebration and post these throughout the school.

Lastly, it is important to be positive and flexible when communicating with the school community and media about your project. Any time they can give you is valuable and better than nothing, and will benefit you and your students.

As you can see, multiple partnerships are essential for quality service-learning projects. The more collaboration and connections you make with your community, the more meaningful the experience will be for everyone involved.

RESOURCE

School/community partnerships selected resources: www.doe.mass.edu/sped/2013/Secondary-Transition/ResourcesFamilyCommunity-Federation.pdf.

Chapter Nine

Working in Teams

Individually we are one drop. Together, we are an ocean. —Ryunosuke Satoro

As Dewey has taught educators, collaborative learning is a valuable way for students to make gains both academically and socially. This does not come without challenges, however, and this chapter will prepare readers for the different stages of development a group can go through during a service-learning project. Discipline suggestions will also be discussed in this section.

The skills: collaboration, teamwork, and communication that come from working together in small groups are essential for our students. The nitty-gritty work of teams is not always easy, but in service learning (as in life) it produces the greatest rewards, products, and process. All groups go through a learning journey together, and, as educators and facilitators, we shepherd them through it, giving support, guidance, and direction as needed. Teachers embarking on service learning for the first time need to know that these teams will struggle, challenge, learn, and eventually grow to be cohesive and functioning. Many will shine and do more than they ever thought they could. Some will be dysfunctional and need close guidance. This is all part of the process. This chapter will tell you what to expect and what to do about problems as they arise.

THE SMALL-GROUP PROCESS

Much has been written about the group process and its phases. In my first service-learning workshop, though, learning about the phases a group goes through was transformative. These were the struggles my own students were going through with every project. So here is a short description of each stage a group can move through. After this, we will explore how this model applies to service-learning groups.

Forming

In service learning, this is the exciting beginning of the project, when students are seeing who their team is and are sharing ideas, exploring possibilities, and learning how they might function together. With elementary, middle, and high school students, there is lots of enthusiastic discussion, interrupting, high-volume discussions, and brainstorms. Often in the forming stage, the sky is the limit. Groups want to take on the world: plant a huge garden to sustain the lunch program, build a greenhouse, create a new program, or choreograph a performance.

Students should be allowed to let their imaginations go wild for the first session, and then guide them to discover what they might be able to accomplish in the given time. Mostly, the facilitator's role in the forming phase is to make sure all students are heard and respected, provide some reality checks, and help students shape their ideas into doable, realistic actions. All the while it will be important to protect their idealistic thinking and grand ideas. This can be a hard line to walk!

Storming

Once students are settled down into the project, likely after a week or so, the reality of what they are doing sinks in. Students begin to realize they need to work hard to achieve their lofty and agreed-upon goals. So they storm. This looks like snippiness between students, role adjusting, agitation, work, and work avoidance. During this phase students are trying to figure out what their role is exactly, and how they fit in.

Some students are used to complaining about a group or group members and then having a teacher solve the problem for them. This might be a teacher deciding on a solution, or giving students the chance to work in alternate teams or on their own. This is not a great way to handle the storming stage. Students here need to learn to persevere. They need to learn to commit and stick with their goals. What a valuable life lesson!

By problem solving with the team, the teacher validates that the team will continue, even with the present challenges. The teacher can meet with the team and openly discuss current issues and guide students to solutions, but not solve it for them. Questions such as "What can this team do to work through this?" and "How can we solve this together?" build a sense of team problem solving and camaraderie.

Students will make it through the storming stage. Most will make it through with limited guidance needed from the teacher, depending on the age

Stage	Tasks	Behaviors
Forming *Polite, but little achieved*	• Establish base expectations • Identify similarities • Agree on common goals • Begin to develop trust	• Getting to know one another and bond • Dependency • Processes often ignored • Rely on leaders for structure, but not full engagement
Storming *Testing others*	• Identify power and control issues • Gain communication skills • Identify resources/balance participation • Begin to build unity	• Express differences of ideas, feelings, and opinions • React emotionally to leadership • Independency or counterdependency • Though under pressure leader needs to be supportive, to listen, to manage conflict, and to explain decisions
Norming *Valuing differences*	• Mutual acceptance • Develop cohesion, commitment, and unity • Team norms, roles, and processes clear and accepted	• Decisions made through negotiation and consensus building • Trust and relationship building • Leader respected and acts as team member, shares leadership, helps build consensus, and enables others
Performing *Flexibility and productivity from trust*	• Achieve challenging, effective, and satisfying results • Find solutions to problems using appropriate controls • Establish autonomy and interdependency	• Collaborative work • Team members care about each other • Team establishes unique identity and behave more strategically • Leader gives projects tasks, and support; team operates on its own

Figure 9.1. Tuckman's Team Development Model *Source: Jim Brenner, professor emeritus, University of California Cooperative Extension, jsbrenner@ucdavis.edu.*

and skillset of the student. Some will need more explicit adult involvement. Soon enough, they will head into the lovely norming and performing stages, and it all will be worth it!

Norming (and Sometimes Even Performing!)

Now the team is humming along with their project, each knowing what to do, and coming together to share and work toward the next goal. Students are positive, engaged, and focused. They are clear on their roles and communicate well with each other. Students are primarily independent in this phase and are building confidence and skills. They usually stay in this phase until the completion of the project. Feeling that level of cooperation and collaboration is empowering and motivating for students, and many great things can be accomplished within these beautiful phases of service learning.

GENERAL GUIDELINES

Of course, your students might not progress through these phases in this order, or they might fall back into one or another (particularly storming!). So, realize that every group is different, just as every learner is different, and their struggles are normal.

Knowing the phases is incredibly helpful because it prepares you for what to expect, generally. If you know that the group is "storming," within limits, you can let them and see if they can work it out. Just knowing these are a normal part of group work can take a lot of pressure off the teacher. When I first started using service learning I found the idea that groups "storm" to be incredibly helpful. I didn't know this was a normal part of group work and the process. So, by framing the work in this way, I was better prepared and able to help my students in these phases.

HIGH-ENERGY GROUPS (WITH STUDENTS WHO HAVE SOME BEHAVIOR ISSUES)

Inevitably, you'll have some high-energy groups that need some attention and guidance with focus issues. Often, the idea of student-led learning is overwhelmingly exciting for these learners. It seems so free that they have a hard time breaking down tasks into meaningful chunks and following through. This is where your role as the facilitator is essential.

For groups that are behaviorally unfocused, you'll need to facilitate their timetable and to-do list. This will need to be guided, with very discrete actions that can be assigned to individuals or partners. Preferably, the first few should be shorter-term actions as well, such as making a phone call, emailing an expert, or getting a question answered through research. That way, these learners find success and engagement in a positive way and learn how the project works. Usually, with guidance and smaller, broken-down tasks, these students are successful.

Occasionally, though, this won't be the case. A student (or two) might be too overwhelmed by the freedom and opportunity a project like this offers. So, clear expectations, small tasks, and the outlining of consequences are necessary. Teachers should use their regular discipline routine with these students. Logical consequences, such as working independently for a set amount of time, are a good motivator. Students want to be involved in these projects. They are exciting, social, engaging, and meaningful. Students who miss out for behavioral reasons often change their behavior so they can be involved again with their team.

In the rare case when this simply doesn't happen, a student can be paired with a paraprofessional or can complete a modified project independently. This is not ideal and every effort to help a student stay in a team should be made, including involvement with parents and the principal. If this is over-whelming for the teacher, and causes the other students to suffer, then this is a last option that can be utilized.

In most cases, you'll find that high-energy, hard-to-focus students will thrive with service learning. In most cases, they simply need a little more direction and involvement. This might mean you'll need more supervision in your classroom. Parent volunteers, special educators, and school support staff can provide some assistance if you need it with this situation.

In some cases, paraprofessionals will already be working with students on Individualized Education Plans (IEPs), or 504 plans (a plan to accommodate a student need or disability) in your classroom. These educational profession-als can work with particular groups where there is a student with a behavioral or academic disability, offering to serve as a mentor to particular teams of students. This support provides the necessary guidance for most students to have great success with service learning.

ONE STUDENTS DOES IT ALL

This is a standard problem in all group work. We've all seen it happen. One student takes over and does most of the work in a group project. One of the main focuses of service learning is for students to develop skills of collabora-tion, teamwork, communication, goal setting, and organization. It benefits no one if one student is doing most of the work and doesn't honor the process.

Luckily, meeting with the involved team is an option that can change this problem quickly. It is essential that the educational leader reads the timeline and "to-do" list, making sure that the jobs are equally distributed. Students might need some guidance here, as assigning tasks is a new skill.

One key part of this problem is for all students to relinquish control of the project to each other. Sometimes, you'll have a perfectionist student, one who wants to succeed and likes to be in charge. This student might need a one-on-one conversation about the nature of the service learning and how group work is essential for the success of the project. There are two common areas of assessment in a model I use for service learning: the portfolio and the project. If a portfolio assessment is used, that will be the individual score for the student. The project is graded separately as a group (or if needed, individually). The portfolio can be a place where a committed, high-achieving student can find the control and personal success they are craving. They obviously can contribute greatly to the project as well, but having two different assessments, one individual and one group, can alleviate some of the self-imposed stress that high-achieving students might be feeling and give them a chance to meet and exceed standards.

High-achieving students can also take on higher-level and more challenging aspects of the project. The facilitation and guidance of the teacher is helpful here; you can guide students in teams to select doable, challenging goals for their particular level and skillset. For example, for one student, writing interview questions for a local judge and then calling or setting up the interview might be overwhelming. But for some, this is the right level of challenge. Use what you know about your students to guide them with proper and logical assignments within their groups.

SPECIAL EDUCATION STUDENTS

It is worth mentioning again that students of all abilities and backgrounds can be successful with service learning. The team aspect, student interest and choice, and the idea of solving community and school problems are very empowering and exciting to most students. In many cases, with the above suggestions, these students will find success within these projects.

To plan for projects with special education students, teachers and special educators should meet prior to the beginning of the project, and throughout it as well, to monitor special education students. Here are some things that have worked to support special education students:

- Find alternative research materials at the student's reading level.
- Provide graphic organizers and other visuals for key concepts.
- Break apart group duties into very specific small steps. Use checklists and cross off tasks as they are accomplished.

- Guide students in positive interactions with the community, school staff, and other students.
- Encourage alternative formats. Most students are used to writing assignments, which can be difficult for students who struggle with reading and writing. They might be surprised and excited to perform a skit, sing a song, or build a model.

The group work in service learning is a dynamic, challenging, and rewarding process for students. It isn't always easy. But together students can accomplish great and meaningful things. They need a teacher who can guide them through the phases and challenges while helping them maintain control and investment in the project. Using these tips can help you make this process smoother and more effective. As you gain experience using service learning with your students, you will develop your own set of group-management techniques that work for your students and learning environment.

Explain that by giving students choice and voice, you are giving them power, privilege, and the knowledge that if they abuse it, they lose it. Help your students realize you are taking a chance by doing unconventional education—you are giving them the benefit of the doubt, the trust, the chance to make a difference. This sets the tone for a collective journey, a collective risk, a collective path that you are on together. Once the students realize this, they will ultimately work harder, dig deeper, and learn more than they ever could have imagined.

RESOURCE

Building Partnerships for Service Learning, B. Jacoby.

Chapter Ten

Authentic Assessments

The difference between school and life? In school, you're taught a lesson and then given a test. In life, you're given a test that teaches you a lesson. —Tom Bodett

Students need to have academic accountability within these projects to meet curricular goals. During this chapter, readers will learn how to create and gather meaningful assessments from the service-learning process. Included will be an example of a portfolio assessment used successfully with my students. This can be modified as a powerful assessment tool for any service-learning project in any content area. There will also be lists and descriptions of multiple and varied assessment opportunities.

Many teachers love the idea of service learning but wonder where the assessment or the evidence of learning is. Assessments for service learning need to be carefully planned to reflect the learning expectations developed. Having various assessments for the project allows teachers to grade various parts of the service-learning experience, to get a full view of the learning journey.

For service learning to be academically successful, it must be firmly rooted in curricular goals and show evidence of learning that can be assessed. This can be done by utilizing several assessments in concert (don't worry—it isn't as hard as you think!). This chapter will describe one successful model and give many ideas for others as well.

THE IMPORTANCE OF ASSESSMENT IN SERVICE LEARNING

Numerous studies have shown that high-quality service learning enhances student learning (Eyler & Giles, 1999), and, in order to do so, this learning needs to be carefully monitored and assessed. According to Steinke and Fitch (2007), "Systematic assessments of service learning provide opportunities to demonstrate the powerful impact that this pedagogy can have on student learning."

Ideally, assessment should happen throughout the project. According to a Vermont Community Works guide to service learning, assessment:

- is complex and multi-dimensional;
- centers on feedback;
- is rooted in context (i.e., situational);
- can be done by the teacher and students;
- is both informal and formal; and
- is ongoing (i.e., it should occur not just when work is done but while students are working and learning). (National Service Learning Assessment Study Group, 1999)

THE PORTFOLIO ASSESSMENT

This is an independent portfolio that each student must complete as part of the project. It contains timelines, vocabulary, education records and activities, information, and built-in reflection about the service-learning project. One portfolio sample is in the appendices for this chapter.

The portfolio is a key piece of assessment because it builds into the project an individual level of accountability. Students know they are each responsible for writing down the timeline, taking notes, listing new vocabulary, and more. By not falling back on one person, or one portfolio, there is an individual accountability and opportunity for each child to succeed. Each student monitors his or her own learning through using this assessment, and teachers can get a clear perspective on the progress of each student throughout the experience.

Depending on their age, students will need reminders and encouragement to work on their portfolios in the project. If used well, it is a guide for the project itself, and contains a record of the individual's whole learning process, from the opening brainstorm to the final reflection.

Possible portfolio parts: You'll find a cover sheet in appendix 10.1 for the portfolio used in my classes (and updated regularly).

It includes:

- learning and brainstorming web;
- planning sheets for the project;
- timeline (to be organized and completed by the team);
- journal entries (for built-in learning reflection);

- project notes and information, which can include: vocabulary sheets, supporting questions, presentation notes, content-area reading notes, research and information, diagrams, drawings and charts; and
- self-assessments: weekly self- and group assessments.

For more information on these parts of a portfolio, see appendix 10.1. You can tailor the portfolio to require any type of learning evidence you would like to see in the project. What if the project is math related? Ask for diagrams and specific math work to support the learning and project. What if it is in Spanish? Have students include writing samples in their portfolios. The portfolio is where you can ask for specific types of learning evidence that will emerge from the project, and if it doesn't, then you can guide students to research or find other learning activities to gain the knowledge to provide these portfolio pieces.

AUTHENTIC ASSESSMENTS (VISUAL AND WRITTEN)

It is recommended that you have at least two components for a project assessment rubric, a written and a visual. This allows for multiple ways to demonstrate learning and knowledge. Service learning has a culminating event, where students share their work. Sharing it in visual and linguistic formats is powerful. Rubrics for these are included in the appendix.

Students can complete projects that have both components. Some examples of combination projects that have both written and visual requirements include:

- a field guide with written species information and pictures of individual species;
- a poster presentation with written information about the topic, with graphs and illustrations;
- a play performance, including the script and the video;
- a garden plot with a guide of plant and seed types, growth patterns, and information;
- a letter-writing campaign with illustrations or pictures of the environmental problem;
- a draft of a bill for the legislature that includes a map of how the bill will pass through various levels of government before becoming law;
- a picture book written by upper-elementary, middle, or high school students for younger grades with detailed text and illustrations;
- a presentation or speech with visual components;
- a presentation with text, images, diagrams, and illustrations (PowerPoint, Google Slides, Prezi, or other);

- writing tasks (interview, letter, press release, report, song or poem, journal, picture book, field guide) shared with the school community;
- a game show (evaluate content with specific criteria); and
- reflection journal with images. (Adapted by Katy Farber and used with permission of Community Works Institute, www. communityworksinstitute.org).

These are just a few ideas from different subject areas; there are countless more. What is key with each of these projects is that you are looking for linguistic and visual learning and processing.

Textbox 10.1
Characteristics of Good Tasks for Standards-Based Learning

- Focus on applying important concepts and essential skills.
- Align with at least one standard.
- Have a real-life application.
- Demand high-level thinking skills (analysis, synthesis, evaluation).
- Culminate in a product that can be scored (e.g., written report, essay, letter, graph, chart, table; speech or multimedia presentation; instruction for a specific audience; a three-dimensional model).
- Allow for multiple types of communication.
- Require more than a simple right or wrong answer.

ASSESSING CIVIC RESPONSIBILITY

One of the strongest gains in service learning is how research links it to the development of students' civic responsibility and engagement. As stated in a previous chapter, students who participate in service learning have higher levels of community engagement and are more likely to volunteer, participate, and vote, and become productive, responsible citizens.

This kind of education is hard to measure, but a few rubrics have been developed to focus on this area. Here is one from Vermont Community Works. In this rubric, a score of 3 meets the standard, and a 4 exceeds the standards. It could also be updated with more positive learning scale language, such as "I can . . ." in place of each number.

ASSESSING ORAL PRESENTATIONS

During a service-learning sharing time, be it a parent night, all-school celebration, or classroom festival, students will have the opportunity to present

Criteria	0 No Demonstration	1 Attempted Demonstration	2 Partial Demonstration	3 Proficient Demonstration	4 Sophisticated Demonstration
Personal	Unaware of responsible personal behavior	Recognizes responsible personal behavior but is unable to explain its importance in a physical activity setting	Able to explain responsible personal behavior but is unable to demonstrate it consistently in a physical activity setting	Able to explain and demonstrate responsible personal behavior in a physical activity setting, including safe and appropriate etiquette and conduct	Able to explain the importance and impact of responsible personal behavior in society
Social	Unable to recognize a competent leader and/or group mentor	Recognizes a competent leader and/or group member, but is unable to identify the skills necessary to function as one	Able to identify the leadership and membership skills necessary to function as a member of a team in a school, family, or community setting and the causes of conflict within these settings	Able to describe and demonstrate the leadership and membership skills necessary to function as a member of a team in a school, family, or community setting and to use strategies to prevent or solve conflict within these settings	Consistently acts as a leader and as a productive group member in a variety of school, family, and/or community settings and incorporates conflict prevention or resolution skills into daily experiences
Civic	Unable to identify a public policy issue in our democracy	Able to identify a public policy issue in our democracy	Able to identify and describe a public policy issue in our democracy	Able to identify and evaluate a public policy issue in our democracy and to explain the importance of active, informed attentive citizen participation in addressing that issue	Actively participates in solving a civic problem and articulates the impact of his/her actions on public policy and constitutional democracy

Figure 10.1. Civic Responsibility Rubric *Adapted by Katy Farber and used with permission of Community Works Institute, www.communityworksinstitute.org.*

their work orally. This is another chance for assessment. Many teachers know students who cannot demonstrate their learning in writing, but they can showcase it beautifully orally. By adding this to your arsenal of assessments, you will have more information about your students' learning, particularly with students who might not demonstrate it otherwise. This is also a chance to assess skills that are featured in different ways in state and national standards and goals, such as the Common Core and Transferrable Skills in Vermont.

There are many great oral presentation rubrics out there. You might have one that works for your students. If not, part of the service-learning project assessment in appendix 10.8 is the presentation criteria. You could use this, use another presentation rubric, or add a presentation component or your overall project rubric. Learning to present orally with good presentation skills is a lifelong skill to master, and students can develop these as well as their content knowledge within service-learning projects.

ASSESSING TEAMWORK

One key element of service learning is how students use their teamwork skills of cooperation, communication, respect, and commitment. Students will be challenged and grow in numerous ways in this area during their projects. They'll need to know that teamwork is part of their assessment and grade and that teams need to work together to succeed. Of course, there will always be challenges in this area, but the key is how students work through it. Utilizing a teamwork rubric to judge this progress and learning is essential. Also, it is helpful if teamwork and collaboration are separate from any content assessments. This way you can view content proficiency separately from other skills. The teacher, volunteers, and students can give feedback about how a team is working (or not working!) together. A teamwork rubric is included in the appendix, and hopefully it works for your class. If not, there are more resources at the end of this chapter.

INVOLVE STUDENTS IN SELF-ASSESSMENT

When you've decided on your assessment plan, and before your launch fully into the project, it is a good idea to go through your assessment (checklist, rubric, scale, or other) in detail with your class. This way students will have a clear idea of what is expected of them. It is even better to have examples of grade-level work to share with your students.

As part of your students' experience with service learning, self-assessment can promote self-analysis, a deeper exploration of learning goals, and a clearer picture of the student's perceptions and learning process.

Explain to students that they will be assessing their own work just as you will be. They will use the same rubrics to grade their work and submit this with their projects. This is particularly helpful with the teamwork rubrics, where students often have strong opinions and insight into the interworking of a group.

When used in this way, self-assessment can be a learning tool and provide more insight for the teacher. In every assessment you use with service learning, I encourage you to have students self-assess their work as well.

Textbox 10.2
Assessment Idea Overview

1. *Teacher observation* could be used to determine how well students master the skills needed for the project.

2. A *rubric* is an excellent way to evaluate student products. Delineating criteria for numerical scales can help clarify expectations for students.

3. Students could use a *checklist* to self-assess their progress in planning the cleanup.

4. A *journal* or *learning log* could be used as a self-assessment tool. Journals also provide a way for students to reflect upon their learning and development cognitive skills.

5. Students could produce a variety of evidence that demonstrates their knowledge and skills. In addition to graphs, students might explain in writing why they chose a particular type of graph. Students might also discuss problems they confronted in their work on this project and how they addressed these. Gathering a wider variety of evidence allows for a more valid and reliable picture of student learning.

Source: The National Service Learning and Assessment Study Group (1999).

TEACH THE RUBRICS, AND USE EXAMPLES

For students to understand the assessments, a few class periods need to be focused on walking through the materials, using examples, modeling behaviors, and allowing for discussion and questions. Read through everything with your students and allow ample time to explain and show examples. Sending copies home to the parents is also a great way to keep them informed about the project and enlist some volunteer assistance.

Rubrics can be tricky when different numbers signify different levels of student achievement. For some rubrics, a 3 is meeting the standard, some 4, and some 5. The numbers are variable. Recent developments in learning scales recommend that numbers should not be used, and words such as *beginning, making progress, proficient*, and *exceeding* should be used instead. Another more positive, child-friendly approach is using the words *getting started, making progress, I can do this*, and *transfer* (Rich, 2016). It is helpful to use one number (or word) system throughout the project, so students and parents don't get confused. Make sure it is clear to students and parents what each number or heading means in a rubric or scale assessment (better yet—label it right on the rubric).

Collecting examples of projects to share with future classes is helpful. This is not possible for those just starting out, but you can start to digitally record the projects so you don't have to collect large projects over the years (save classroom space!). You can do this with digital photography, with videos, or on class websites. In fact, many schools are now moving to personalized learning plans, websites, and blogs to house the assessments, reflection, and project sharing in service and project-based learning. (These tools will be further explored in chapter 13).

The Responsive Classroom model of classroom management works very well as a whole-class or as a whole-school program. It also ties in very nicely with service learning. Responsive Classroom "is an approach to elementary teaching that emphasizes social, emotional, and academic growth in a strong and safe school community. The goal is to enable optimal student learning. Created by classroom teachers and backed by evidence from independent research, the Responsive Classroom approach is based on the premise that children learn best when they have both academic and social-emotional skills. The approach therefore consists of classroom and school wide practices for deliberately helping children build academic and social-emotional competencies" (Responsive Classroom, 2010). This type of organizational structure in a classroom provides students with a social framework to engage in the work of service learning.

The process of developing a strong class community will only help facilitate more powerful and enriching service-learning projects with your students.

Teachers have known that service learning, students solving community problems, is a motivating and rich tool for learning. What has been harder is for teachers to quantify this learning. By establishing learning goals and developing tools to assess them, teachers can not only justify the merit and worth of service-learning projects but also guide students to more specific and clear learning outcomes. By using the tools and ideas in this chapter, I hope you have a better sense of how you can plan service-learning assessments more easily.

RESOURCES

Service   Learning   and   Assessment: A   Field   Guide   for   Teachers:
www.communityworksinstitute.org/cwpublications/slassessguide/slassessguide.html.
Menu of resources on service learning, including assessments: http://www.
communityworksinstitute.org/cwpublications/slassessguide.html.

Chapter Eleven

Powerful Reflection

A mind that is stretched by a new experience can never go back to its old dimensions. —Oliver Wendell Holmes

Reflection is an integral part of service and project-based learning. As in education, with our fast pace, increasing expectations, and sense of urgency, it is something that is often overlooked. For students engrossed in service learning, reflection opportunities provide a chance to think about this new on-the-ground real-life learning. And the results are powerful. It just takes time and specific opportunities encouraged by the teacher.

Luckily, there are many ways to provide reflection to your students during the unit, and they don't have to take much time from the project itself. Each teacher should find what works for them. Consider frequency, format, and duration. Below are some of the ideas I have seen that work well.

BEST PRACTICES FOR DESIGNING REFLECTION

When creating reflection opportunities in your service-learning projects, it is helpful to keep these guidelines in mind. From www.servicelearning.org:

Reflection activities work best when they are designed well, planned in advance, and implemented thoughtfully. Reflection is a continuous process and activities can occur at any time during the process. Effective reflection incorporates the following best practices:

- Reflection should occur before the service-learning experience, during the experience, and after the experience.
- Reflection activities should clearly link the service-learning experience to academic standards and curriculum objectives.

- Frequent opportunities for discussion of service should be provided so students can interact with their peers, mentors, and those they serve.
- Reflection activities should challenge students to test assumptions about their values and to explore, clarify, and alter their values.
- Students should be included in the planning of reflection activities so that they have ownership of the process.
- Reflection activities should incorporate various learning styles (visual, auditory, kinesthetic) and experiences to encourage students to think in different ways.
- Teachers should provide continual feedback to students so they can improve their critical thinking and analytical skills during the reflective process. (www.servicelearning.org/instant_info/fact_sheets/k-12_facts/reflection/expanded)

OPPORTUNITIES FOR REFLECTION

During service and project-based learning, you can provide frequent, informal reflection opportunities for your students rather easily. It is helpful during this times to take notes on the students' discussion and reflections so you can provide feedback for students to improve. A combination of the ideas below is recommended for use during your service-learning projects with students. Here are a few ways to provide these short but meaningful opportunities for reflection:

- Small-group check-ins: When students are engaged in small-group project work, the teachers, support staff, and even parent volunteers can visit with groups and check in about their progress. Ask students to reflect on what is working and what they need help with, and ask detailed questions about their particular project. This will provide small snippets of reflection (see small-group reflection question ideas in appendix 7.1).
- Whole-class big questions: At the end of class, it is a good idea to gather the whole class and share reflections on the group work and learning as a whole group. This way, students can learn from each other that it is normal to be working out difficult problems and challenges, and to share any interesting or inspiring knowledge gained from working on their projects. This also allows for groups to cross collaborate.
- One group, for example, might be working on developing a wildflower garden and another on butterfly habitats. These teams can work together and share information if they are aware of the work the other group is doing. A list of general whole-class reflection questions is listed in appendix 7.2.
- One-on-one discussions: These are a great way to see how an individual student is developing in the service-learning process. It is particularly helpful to check in with both low- and high-achieving students to gauge

their involvement, needs, and participation in the project. Students are sometimes more receptive to speaking about challenges in a one-on-one setting.

- As much as possible, document these discussions. It will help you with your all-around assessment, to troubleshoot, and to monitor the learning and reflection happenings with students. I like to have one notebook that I carry around during group work, and either I will have support staff give me feedback that I write down in this notebook, or they write it down and I attach it within. This is also a great place to record your reflections about the project.
- Student journals: There are many ways to use journals for service-learning reflection. It can be a powerful reflection tool. I suggest a balance of the different types of journal entries below. These can be included in a portfolio assessment (as described in chapter 7), or as a standalone assessment and reflection.
- Students can free write, or respond to a list of prompts (see the list of journal prompts at the end of this chapter).
- Students focus on new learning (one thing you learned, a diagram to support it, and a connection you made)—one due every week.
- Assign specific journal assignments for older students (thought-provoking, critical-thinking questions).
- Sketchbooks: These can be used in conjunction with verbal and written reflection to provide opportunities for students to use their multiple intelligences. Students may need to draw designs for projects, diagrams from their research, or images that reflect their new learning and teamwork process.
- Question or big idea list: Often during these projects, students think of many more questions. And they often come to big ideas and conclusions in their work. These can be recorded on a page (see appendix 8.4) and reflected on with a small or large group.
- Technology tools: Now with many schools going 1:1 with computers or iPads, there are even more opportunities for reflection. Students can use photos, video, and other tools for reflection. See chapter 13 for specific examples of helpful technology tools to support reflection in service and project-based learning.

In a portfolio used for assessment, reflections can be embedded. Weekly team reflections can show problem areas as well as the personal development of a student (see appendix 8.2).

Unit reflections also give a window into the thinking of students at the end of a service-learning experience. This can be invaluable as the teacher reflects and plans for the next service-learning project, and to help communicate to parents how the student was feeling about his or her work.

Textbox 11.1

More Ideas for Student Reflection

Classroom Journal: In this exercise, students reflect upon their classmates' and teacher's journal entries. Prompt your students by writing the first entry. Then, each day, have a different student take the journal home and write an entry that reflects upon the most recent contribution before their own.

Community Journal: A community journal is one that the students share with the community agency staff or community members during a service-learning project. At the agency or work site, students ask community members to add an entry to the journal about their project experience or work at the agency. To get the ball rolling, you should prompt the community members with journaling ideas. Try to collect as many community entries as there are students in your class. After the service-learning project is over, assign students different community entries upon which to reflect and respond.

Classroom Discussions: These can be one of the most stimulating forms of reflection for service learning. Discussing real-world issues and themes that are relevant to the service-learning project provides students with an opportunity to explore critical thinking skills, communication skills, and current events with their peers.

Here are a few suggestions for making your classroom discussions more exciting and productive:

1. Invite a community representative to lead the discussion.
2. Have each student take a turn at leading the discussion.
3. Cut out articles from the newspaper that relate to the service-learning project and have the students discuss the broader issues that are involved.
4. Videotape each discussion and make a reflective video at the end of the project, so that students remember the issues discussed and the results of each discussion.
5. Have each student bring an object related to the service-learning project (tool, photograph, etc.) to the discussion and share the relevance of the object to their service-learning experience.

Visual Arts

Another way to introduce reflection into your classroom in a more creative way. Paint and paper or digital media can be very compelling mediums for both younger and older students to express their thoughts about their service-learning experiences. Any of these ideas can help get you started:

Photographic Journal: Instead of having students simply write in journals, have them take photographs of the service-learning project and write journal entries in response to the photographs they have taken.

Project Website: Many students have a real knack for website design. As your project progresses, have the students create a website so that their service-learning project can be shared in cyberspace with parents, students, community members, and project partners.

Bulletin Boards: School bulletin boards that are in public areas of the school can be a great way for students to share their service-learning project with the student body, teachers, and school administration.

Have your class adopt one of the school's bulletin boards and keep everyone updated about what is going on with service-learning. Students can take pictures of the project and post them, as well as post other literature related to the project, such as thank-you letters from community members written in response to the project.

Source: Adapted from Pennsylvania Service Learning Alliance (2002–2007).

There are many resources available to educators about leading reflections with your students throughout the service-learning process. It can be overwhelming. Below I picked a few resources in case you need more ideas and resources than this book offers. Also, please refer back to chapter 2 on project-based learning for more ideas about reflection.

By providing both informal and quick reflection opportunities, and more formal, culminating reflections, you will provide deeper learning experiences for your students and have more of an effect on their lives. Reflection makes service learning richer for students and provides valuable feedback for teachers. This, in turn, can help teachers reflect on the service-learning process and improve their practice the next time around.

RESOURCES

Handout about the importance of reflection in service learning, www2.smc.edu/servicelearn-
ing/reflection%20handout.doc.
The 40 Reflection Questions, www.edutopia.org/pdfs/stw/edutopia-stw-replicatingPBL-
21stCAcad-reflection-questions.pdf.
Facilitating Reflection: A Manual for Educators, www.uvm.edu/~dewey/reflection_manual.

Chapter Twelve

Securing Funding

We refuse to believe that there is insufficient funds in the great vaults of
opportunity of this nation. —Dr. Martin Luther King Jr.

Too many times educators hear "in these difficult economic times" or "these
tough economic times" as an excuse for defunding schools. Back in 2010
during the writing of the first edition of this book, we were in the worst
recession since the Great Depression, and everyone was suffering. And
schools took a direct hit. Programs were cut, budgets slashed, and teachers
were laid off. None of this was easy or in the best interest of students. While
our economy has recovered, schools still face budget challenges and cuts.

So educators who want to do this revolutionary work have to think creatively to make it happen. The good thing is, it doesn't have to cost much.
And with some planning, teachers can cover any expenses during projects
pretty easily.

What sort of costs come up? Small groups might want to plant a garden,
make signs, perform a play, or create a book, to list only a few examples.
These activities usually take some specific materials to make them happen
fully. This chapter will help you figure out how to get these materials at a
minimal cost.

SCHOOL-BASED FUNDING

School-based funding is by far the best way to ensure consistent funding for
service-learning projects. At budgeting time, teachers build materials and
supplies into their classroom budgets, just as a teacher would for pencils,
books, paper, and other supplies.

Many principals are excited and motivated about service learning and will support adding funds for these materials in their budgets. This takes meeting with your principal during budgeting time and advocating for these funds. How much? That depends on the number of students, the duration of the project, and the scope, of course. But estimating about five hundred dollars for about twenty-five students is a good place to start.

Some principals are reluctant to support budgeting changes or increases. Showing them the many ways service learning improves academic success and civic engagement, decreases the dropout rate, and increases school attendance (see chapter 3), can convince them. You might need to do a presentation for the school board about service learning. (Don't slam this book shut! It's not that bad!) You can use the data from this book, and the resources listed at the end of the book (and each chapter) to help you. They will likely be convinced of service learning's greatness and fund your work fully.

If not, don't fear; there are other options.

Raise the Resources

This isn't as daunting as it sounds. There are several options to help you raise money or find materials for your service-learning projects.

Parent Donations

In your class newsletters and on your website, you could simply write about your planned project and ask for donations. This way, parents with fewer economic resources won't feel as if they have to contribute, but those who are comfortable and willing might donate just what you need. You know your community, their economic levels, and how they might react to this, so this may be a tool you use or ultimately skip altogether.

Homegrown Fundraisers

You know what I am talking about—bake sales, car washes, and the like. You can organize and run one of these. If you find your projects in need of materials, getting them could be as easy as requesting students to bake something and bring it to the next basketball game for a bake sale. Of course, if the project is huge, you'll have to coordinate a much larger effort.

Homegrown fundraisers that link to projects are terrific, too, such as building birdhouses to sell to support an environmental set of projects. Parents are usually willing to help out, materials can be donated, and everyone can meet on a Saturday to create something of value, such as birdhouses, pasta sauce, bat boxes, or any other creative ideas.

These fundraisers are wonderful because they are linked to communities and their needs. You can utilize your community contacts and resource people to help generate ideas for small fundraisers to support your projects.

Environmental Fundraisers for Schools

Many great programs have popped up in the last several years to help schools with fundraising. It is much easier for busy teachers and small groups to raise funds than ever before.

Magazine or candy sales do not seem in line with the goals of service learning, healthy living, and local communities. There are green and sustainable fundraising organizations that are worth looking into if you are undertaking a very large project and would like to have full funding in place before you begin.

Environmental fundraising groups: These organizations help schools by supplying environmentally friendly projects such as fair-trade coffee and chocolate, no-waste lunch kits, and reusable water bottles. Schools take a significant portion of the profits, and are promoting greener lifestyles in the process.

- **Equal Exchange:** Fair trade products (including chocolate) instead of wrapping paper and magazines? Yes, please.
- **MightyNest:** This hub of green products has a school fundraising division that hosts school fundraising with a focus on healthy schools and kids.
- **Terracycle:** This organization promotes recycling of hard-to-recycle items in schools and offers a portion of the profits back to schools. A win-win.
- **More ideas are found here at Green Child Magazine:** www.greenchildmagazine.com/eco-friendly-fundraising.

Local Businesses and Banks

Many local businesses and banks are happy to support schools, especially if they can gain some good marketing out of it. In one service-learning project where students created a community magazine, the students sold local businesses advertising space to fund the project. It might just take a visit from a few students to motivate local businesses to contribute to a school-community project.

Local Rotary or Kiwanis Clubs

These clubs often participate in charitable donations to the community. Often they have community donations written into their budgets and want to support meaningful work. A well-written letter to a club about the project might yield significant funding and community involvement.

COMMUNITY-BASED GRANTS

Take a look at your local nonprofits. What ones exist to support schools? To support the local environment? Or civic engagement? Likely there is an organization supporting the kind of work you intend to do. All it takes might be a call explaining your project and what kind of support you need.

Ask your principal and superintendent if they are aware of any local groups; then try the community pages of your phone book for contacts. This is likely not something you want to spend your time doing as a busy teacher. Truthfully, you might not even need to with the other funding options—but if you need to, you can. Someone on your school staff is likely to know about a group that might support your work as well, so mention it at a staff meeting (or in an email).

For a few years, a local nonprofit would supply my class with just enough funds necessary to get the materials for student groups. Sometimes you might be in the middle of work on projects with students and discover a financial need. Then you can inquire, explain what the funds are for, and usually be granted the funds. This was my experience.

There are larger, more corporate grants available as well. Here is a list of those, but this is only a preliminary search—there are countless more. It is a starting point if you need to look into this kind of funding.

Funding sources includes:

Youth Service America: www.ysa.org/grants
Toyota Tapestry Grants: www.nsta.org/pd/tapestry
Corporation for National and Community Service: www.nationalservice. gov/build-your-capacity/grants/funding-opportunities

MAKE DO WITH WHAT YOU HAVE

Here is a little secret—aside from the support my class received for my first few years in service learning, our class has not received any outside funds other than from parents, or from within the school. And in our current economic reality, most teachers will find themselves in this boat. We are forever resourceful, teachers, and often must simply make do with what we have (or don't have).

Schools have loads of stuff. Stuff in storage, in closets, out of sight, or piled high. In many cases, it is a matter of finding what you need. So I often send emails to the staff requesting this or that, and most materials have appeared in a matter of days. The custodian is also one to maintain a strong appreciation for and relationship with. He or she can point you to tons of gear you might need for your students' work. For us, it was shovels, a wheelbarrow, and some soil, or signposts, wood, and paint. This kind of reuse is environmentally responsible as well!

Parents and volunteers are often able to lend materials, or buy a few for groups. And the longer you do this, the more materials your classroom will have to be ready for the next year (just be ready to ask for that storage shed out back).

If you have older students, too, funding can be part of their projects and their jobs. High school students can realize what they need and develop a way to get it. How compelling it is when articulate and dedicated high school students request funding from the principal! Any way you can release responsibility back to the students will make a richer experience with more buy-in and ownership from the students.

So don't let your budget woes or a lack of funding stop you from service learning. In most cases, you can do it without much financial support. If you find yourself needing some funding for your students, don't fear; just try one of the ideas listed above and you will likely get what you need.

Idea list for doing with what you have:

- Contact your custodian.
- Contact your school staff.
- Contact your school administration.
- Contact parents.
- Contact community members.
- Check in storage areas for what you need.
- Look on Freecycle.com for what you need.
- Look on Craigslist.com for what you need.
- Contact your local solid waste company and tell them what your needs are in case someone has recently thrown out usable supplies (hardware, wood, nails, etc.).

There are many resources out there to support your great work in service learning. Start with your own school and community, and then reach out if you find a need with your service-learning projects. People love to support real and meaningful work with children in their own communities.

Chapter Thirteen

Technology Tools That Support Project-Based and Service Learning

The technology itself is not transformative. It's the school, the pedagogy, that is transformative. —Tanya Byron

While teaching during the first edition of this book (all the way back in 2010!), we used paper for most things in school. The first edition advocated for using a paper portfolio to document the learning during service-learning projects. While paper still has a role to play, technology has given us (and especially students) an exciting opportunity as a tool to develop creative products, to collaborate, to create scaffolds, and to document and share student work. What follows is a review of the technological tools that can help support both service and project-based learning. This will likely grow and change rapidly, so be sure to visit the resource websites linked at the bottom to stay up to date about the new resources and tools being created. Thankfully, we are entering a time when technology tools can help students and teachers tell the stories of their learning, and make these stories available to the world. To frame this section, consider this quote by Alan November: "Teachers need to stop saying, 'Hand it in,' and start saying 'Publish It.'"

Technology tools are here to help students create and publish their own work to a wider audience. This will create authentic audiences, engagement, and relevance for students in this digital age.

GOOGLE SITES

The first iteration of Google Sites was challenging to work with. Thankfully, there is a new version (as of 2017) that is much easier to use and also very professional looking. Google Sites can be used as a frame to house service and project-based learning. Teachers can set up one site for each project, and pages within that site to indicate phases of projects and link to the phases and supports needed. For example, one Google Site was created for fourth grades in an elementary school. They were studying the town's history. The teacher set up pages within the site that included:

- Question (the driving or focusing questions)
- Research (graphic organizers, curated sites, note-taking tools)
- Script (for videos they made)
- Presentation (assignment, rubrics, and expectations)
- Resources
- Student work (a place to post final projects)

Google Sites are also a great way to make your work transparent and sharable to your school community. Parents can easily access components of the project, follow along, and provide support. It is also helpful to have an online home for the project when reaching out to the community for partnerships, resources, or an authentic audience. You can link to the site to give partners a feel for the project, class, and students.

LAUNCHPAD

Google Sites is not the only way to organize a project. A new app called LaunchPad does the same, but allows for much more robust teacher collaboration, planning, resource linking, and sharing with students. It is a very visual way to organize your service or project-based learning. It is essentially like Pinterest for projects, but with a built-in framework that teachers can fill in collaboratively to create projects. Eventually, teachers will be able to copy and modify existing projects, and collaborate with team teachers in their schools, or teachers anywhere in the world. There is great potential here. This could be used in conjunction with a Google (or presentation type) site. The planning and sharing with students could be done in LaunchPad, and the sharing and public site could be a Google Site. Both of these resources provide much-needed organization and support for this type of learning. They are online, collaborative, and linked binders of projects and ideas.

PADLET

Padlet is essentially an online and fully linked way to step up sticky notes. This tool creates a little visual snapshot of whatever is being shared, and you can arrange them in any order you like. If given permission, students can also post on the boards. So for service and project-based learning, you can create one or several Padlets to share on the Smartboard and with students. You can use this to brainstorm project ideas, to share curated resources with students, to show a progression of steps, and to organize student reflection, presentations, tasks, and so on. This tool is simple to use and provides an easy way to organize links, documents, and ideas.

ADOBE SPARK

Adobe Spark is a relatively new way for students to create beautiful, visual stories. These can be created with or without voiceover screen casting. Pictures, videos, and text can be integrated on this web tool. These become sharable, visual documentation of projects. Right now it is available only to kids over thirteen, so if using with younger students, a teacher has to set up an account and have students log in and create Sparks in that account. Students can design these online stories in teams, with a focus on a community problem, or they can tell a story with photographs about their community as a service and share these. The ideas are endless with this tool!

PINTEREST

As many educators know, Pinterest has a wealth of ideas for the classroom. Sometimes all it takes to spark an idea with teachers or students embarking on this work is to see images of similar projects. Pinterest is loaded with creative ideas for projects, motivational tools and tips, visual ways to share projects, and organizing tools for teachers.

IMOVIE

Students love working with video! iPads and iMovie make a powerful tool for service and project-based learning. Students can use these tools to create products for any project. They can host film festivals, create how-to videos, host newscasts, interview community members, enliven historical resources and sites, you name it. Here are three types of videos that can be used in service- and project-based learning that can motivate and engage students, and that work well in showcasing content areas (first published at the Tarrant Institute for Innovative Education blog; Farber, 2016e):

How-To Videos

How-to videos are a great way to showcase research or demonstrate proficiency with a new skill. After all, the best way to demonstrate mastery of a skill is by teaching others. Some ideas for how-to videos include:

- solving math or chemistry equations (students teaching students is sometimes more effective than teachers);
- parallel parking (problem-based learning in driver's education!);
- how to safely use a Bunsen burner (beginning of a science class);
- computer skills (these could be shared with the elderly as a service);
- construction, STEM, or engineering projects (what are the steps?);
- sustainability projects, such as caring for chickens or building a pond; and
- writing a poem.

This can work particularly well with math. Students can create Khan Academy–style videos to share with younger students. They could even create a Google Site that features these videos for younger (or even absent) students.

Interviews

Interview-style videos give students a motivating way to analyze facts and opinions around a specific content area. Formats for these can include setting up a mock debate or simulation, or pursuing more in-depth learning around a topic by actually setting up an interview with a content area expert. For example, students could plan a town meeting where mock legislation is being proposed. A video team could film this and interview the participant. Or, during a mock trial, the video team could interview various participants in their various roles including lawyers, the jury, the judge, and witnesses. Students can also brainstorm interview questions for community members around a theme. Themes could include telling the story of a community, listening to the elders, careers, opinions about any issue, and storytelling. There are many possibilities for intersections with this tool.

Newscasts

This format is very popular with students! This is an extremely engaging way to motivate students, and all students have seen this kind of reporting. Making video newscasts is a great way for students to try out video journalism, and assembling content-based scripts helps make those newscasts powerful and reflects deeper, integrated learning. There are many apps that can replicate the green screen used in news casting, as well as green screen equipment available in many school systems.

For links to examples of these projects, and more content specific ideas for videos, please see the resources at the bottom of this chapter.

PROJECT CALENDARS

Everyone likes to be organized, especially teachers. Using an online calendar for project planning can help the project feel more manageable. You can set up a Google calendar just for your project and share it with students by projecting it to a Smartboard, or sharing it with them online. If you start with the culminating event in mind, and plan backward to the beginning of the unit (leaving a little wiggle room for any delays), then you can get an idea of how you can time the project on the calendar.

THINGLINK

Another interesting technology tool is Thinglink. This is a way to feature a visual image and embed links into it. This can be used in many ways, including mapping, biographies, exploring themes in literature, and projects in any subject. These can then be easily shared as part of a larger project or as a standalone project, and featured online.

As soon as this book is published, there are likely to be several new tools to add to this list. We live in a time where more tools are becoming available, and students want to use them. Hopefully this chapter shows you that there are many ways technology can enhance service and project-based learning.

RESOURCE

This post at the Tarrant Institute for Innovative Education features the above tools with embedded examples and content-area ideas: http://tiie.w3.uvm.edu/blog/videos-for-showcasing-content-areas/#.WEq_9KIrKwQ.

Chapter Fourteen

Makerspaces and Genius Hours

The future belongs to the curious. The ones who are not afraid to try it, explore it, poke at it, question it, and turn it inside out. —Anonymous

Service and project-based learning are not the only games in town that can transform education. While these are powerful pedagogies, there are other approaches that share some of the same core values that can engage, excite, and motivate students while connecting them to their communities and interests. Here are two such approaches, and there are many other versions of them as well, with helpful resources for developing and extending each one.

MAKERSPACES

There is a Makerspace movement afoot in education and it is exciting. Many libraries have computer labs that are no longer needed because of 1:1 in-classroom computers or iPads. This space is perfect for creating a Maker-space for tinkering and creating. Many librarians and media specialists have started creating these spaces with and for students.

Just what is a Makerspace? Like most concepts in education, definitions vary. There is a wonderful post about these many definitions listed in the resources below, but in summary, Makerspaces provide the space, time, tools, and support for students to tinker, create, and make things. Lest you think you have to have a 3D printer to create a Makerspace, this quote helps show that it is not the tools alone that make the space:

Makerspaces come in all shapes and sizes, but they all serve as a gathering point for tools, projects, mentors and expertise. A collection of tools does not define a Makerspace. Rather, we define it by what it enables: making. (Maker-space, 2013)

101

So what could it look like?

- One day a week in math class asking students to meet a design challenge or math concept with found materials such as Legos, sewing craft materials, cardboard, electronics, and building supplies.
- A classroom or shared space where materials are collected and sorted into bins and used for weekly challenges, open creating times, or specific projects.
- Cardboard-only Makerspaces. As part of the cardboard online challenge, students can create an arcade, models of buildings, airplanes, or rockets and invite other classes to come and visit these creations.
- Robotics equipment clubs and challenges.
- Shop classes are now Education Technology, STEM, or STEAM classes. These are woodworking, mechanical, pre-engineering, or vocational classes and are definitely Makerspaces.
- Let students lead the way. My colleague at the Tarrant Institute of Innovative Education wrote a post about involving students in the creation of a Makerspace to promote excitement and ownership and shares steps for how to do just that. (Legeros, 2016a)

When pondering how to create or extend a Makerspace, it is important to consider specific design elements. Led by Life Legeros, the Tarrant Institute for Innovative Education professional development coordinators created a Makerspace design feature continuum. This focuses on:

- the amount of structure in the opportunities;
- the amount of student involvement in the setup and operation;
- community member involvement;
- the document plans for student experiences;
- curriculum connections;
- how much technology will be involved;
- how long and sustained the projects are; and
- connections (or not) to the greater good. Based on my research I encourage Makerspace creations to have some purpose toward the greater good.

See the Makerspace design features document linked below for resources and ideas about each of these design elements. Even if you have no space for a Makerspace, you can gather some materials (even just cardboard) and give the space, time, and support for creating. Luckily, Makerspaces are exploding (thankfully not literally) across our nation's schools and there are many resources to inspire and guide you. Grab a couple of colleagues, and brainstorm what it could look like in your school and community. Makerspace creator Jen Hill of Crossett Brook Middle School did just that. She found herself with an open space, and worked with school staff and her students to create a grassroots Makerspace. To get inspired, she visited a local art studio of a known maker and artist, the Generator Makerspace in Burlington, and the MIT Inventeams Makerspace (Hill, 2016). These informed her work in creating a Makerspace with and for students at her middle school. See the full post below with embedded videos for your own inspiration. And like any maker, she is thinking about next steps for their Makerspace. Based on my research, Makerspaces should connect to the greater good for the school and community. What can students make that will help someone? What can they make that will help solve a community or school problem? This next step in connecting to a greater purpose is combining the realms of the maker movement with service learning and can be very powerful for students and the communities where they live.

This is only the beginning! Rest assured, though, if you are unable to create a Makerspace in some way in your class, you can infuse elements of it into your service or project-based learning work with students by allowing them the freedom, support, and flexibility to create, do, and make in the classroom.

GENIUS HOUR

A concept that traces back to Google, and has been also referred to as "20 percent time," is Genius Hour. It is a simple idea. Google encouraged its employees to take 20 percent of their weekly work time and devote it to projects of their own interest. The result? Innovations such as Gmail or Google News. Author Daniel Pink also referred to companies that are using this concept and getting innovative results from employees (Pink, 2016).

In Education, Genius Hour blossomed with the publication of several books and articles linking Google's 20 percent time concept with the concept of providing a Genius Hour for students, or sixty minutes each week where students get to direct their own learning. The authors of *The Genius Hour Guidebook* define Genius Hour in education as

> an inquiry-driven, passion-based classroom strategy designed to excite and engage students through the unrestrained joy of learning. We (and many other Genius Hour teachers) accomplish this by setting aside time in our weekly classroom schedules when students are able to learn about and create whatever they want, unencumbered by teacher control. (Zvi & Krebs, 2016)

While this is an exciting development in many schools, elements of Genius Hour are embedded in service and project-based learning, specifically student voice and choice, student self-direction, and project creation. In more traditional schools, Genius Hour can provide a way to motivate and engage students in creative work. In schools that already feature service and project-based learning, but it is more teacher directed in terms of curricular content, Genius Hour can provide a forum for students to explore their own interests free from curricular expectations. Having Genius Hour in the schedule also shows that schools value creative time and it will happen regularly, versus time that can get absorbed into other priorities.

University of Vermont professor and director of the Tarrant Institute of Innovative Education Penny Bishop wrote an interesting critique of Genius Hour. She posits that the danger of relying solely on sixty minutes a week for student self-direction and creativity is a bit like studying women's history and black history only during those special months. She said,

> For 60 minutes, students are engaged, they have choice, and they are following their passion. Yet, just as Black History Month relieves schools during the other months from seriously considering how an entire group of people was summarily excluded from America's history books, so too can Genius Hour free schools up to devote the many other hours of the day to the kind of rote learning and test-taking we know to be both ineffective and disengaging. (Bishop, 2014)

Hopefully, Genius Hours are only the start of engaging students based on their interests and it can extend beyond the sixty-minute-per-week concept and guidelines. Indeed, practitioners of Genius Hour have noted that much like service and project-based learning, the benefits and learning extend well beyond deemed project times.

When considering starting a Genius Hour, there are several design elements to ponder. These were created by Life Legeros at the Tarrant Institute for Innovative Education and cultivated by our team of professional development coordinators. The Google Document shares many resources to consider as well; a link is provided in the "Resources" section at the end of this chapter.

Genius Hour design elements:

- How much upfront planning will be necessary?
- Project calendars
- Mentorships
- Requirements for end products
- Student reflection
- Assessing student work
- Curriculum connections
- Student involvement in various aspects of planning and sharing projects

One caution for Genius Hour is to avoid the pitfall of over-"schoolifying" the time with templates, plans, and teacher directedness (Legeros, 2016b).

This can kill creativity and motivation. Find ways for students to co-construct any rubrics, checklists, and plans for project sharing. This will lead to more involvement and buy-in from students.

A middle school in central Vermont, Crossett Brook, created a Genius Hour called Brainado. It was scheduled one hour a week, for ten weeks, and here are some of the things that the students produced:

- engineering and building a working hover board;
- creating a scale model of Real Madrid's soccer stadium;
- hatching chickens;
- investigating the throwing power of various lacrosse sticks;
- "singing" a Beyoncé song using sign language;
- filming the process of training a miniature horse;
- organizing a fun run to raise funds for an annual community event;
- designing and sewing a custom-made dress for a friend; and
- dehydrating meals for a week-long backpacking trip. (Legeros, 2016b)

The power of programs like Brainado is the impact it can have across the school, and how the approach to valuing student voice and interests can reverberate across curriculum, instruction, and the school community. According to Legeros (2016b):

> Most importantly, Brainado has become a touchstone for the entire school community as we strive to increase student engagement and deepen learning. We now have a shared experience that provides a shorthand to ask questions such as "how do we capture the energy of Brainado in our day-to-day classrooms" or "how can Personalized Learning Plans be more like Brainado?"

Infusing school with hands-on work—be it in project-based learning, service learning, Genius Hour, or Makerspaces—will likely only increase student engagement and motivation and provide authentic opportunities for student personal growth. These educational approaches have overlapping themes: more student self-direction, more creativity, more problem solving, and more connections to the community and student engagement. These are the ways that we can prepare students for life in the twenty-first century and to lead a creative, engaged, civic life.

RESOURCES

5 Ways to Partner with Students in a Makerspace: http://tiie.w3.uvm.edu/blog/partner-with-students-in-a-Makerspace/#.WGqq9LYrLrI.
Makerspace Design Features: https://docs.google.com/document/d/1OOUezK_PrTfqkfonaudyEXHtNW2PY—N_46fflARlmI/edit?usp=sharing.
Youth Makerspace Playbook (full of helpful ideas and resources): http://makered.org/wp-content/uploads/2015/09/Youth-Makerspace-Playbook_FINAL.pdf.

Chapter 14

Makerspace example with videos: http://tiie.w3.uvm.edu/blog/the-story-of-Makerspace/#.WHJXfLYrL_8.

Genius Hour design features: https://docs.google.com/document/d/1Hhbi-3yaGXPkKFBCL1_6xz4JhYTsR8GUUtjs-Mz70f0/edit.

Genius Hour example, Brainado, with lots of resources: http://tiie.w3.uvm.edu/blog/brainado/#.WHJcnrYrL_8.

Chapter Fifteen

Voices from the Field

*Inspiration, Advice, and Guidance
from Teachers Currently Leading Project-Based and
Service Learning Programs*

Listen and learn from people who have already been where you want to go.
Benefit from their mistakes instead of repeating them. —Benjamin Carson

There are so many teachers across this country doing amazing work in the
area of service and project-based learning. From them you will find inspiration, words of wisdom, and practical advice. For this section five teachers
from different regions of the United States and different subject areas were
interviewed to give you a sense of what some teachers are doing with their
students. This is only a beginning—there are thousands of teachers across the
country doing this type of work.

Take what you can from them. Teachers need to share with each other,
listen to each other, and inspire each other in this important work.

CREATING A COMMUNITY RESOURCE AND PROMOTING
HEALTHY LIVING

Here is an interview from a seventh-grade social studies teacher, Marlo Den-
tice, with additional support from Sarah Bush. You'll see how he integrated
service learning with his social studies curriculum, provided for reflection,
and didn't require much funding to do so.

1. Provide a brief description/narrative of your project (include purpose/goals, a brief timeline, the "story").

A few seventh graders had asked me if our class could participate in the WE The People program. WE The People . . . Project Citizen introduces students to and educates them in the methods and procedures used in our political process.

The goal of the program is to develop students' commitment to active citizenship and governance by providing the knowledge and skills required for effective participation, providing practical experience designed to foster a sense of competence and efficacy, and developing an understanding of the importance of citizen participation. This program helps the students' knowledge, enhances their skills, and deepens their understanding of how "the people"—all of us—can work together to make communities better. This project started in September and it ended in May where the students presented their project at the capital [Madison].

2. What opportunities were available for youth leadership and voice?

This project was completely the students' idea. A few students had approached me about participating in this program. The program is completely student-centered, student-directed. I explained the project to them and gave them a timeline, but they decided how much they wanted to participate. I was just the supervisor that helped guide the students and made sure they were on the right track. I helped mediate the conversations and voting but the students are the ones that researched, wrote letters, and made phone calls. They challenged themselves each and every day, making this project the great success it was.

3. What "community" need did this project address?

In the program, the students decide as a class what problem they would like to address in their community. The students really focused on the development of a public policy to deal with a specific problem in the community and the recommendation of that policy to the appropriate government or governmental agency.

As a class, the students voted on working on cleaning up the wooded area between Canterbury Elementary School and Greendale Middle School. The students decided they would try to clean up the area in the woods so that students would stop drinking and smoking or even doing drugs in the woods. The students thought by getting the police involved and constructing disc-golf in the woods there would be more people in the woods, hopefully scaring off drug users, and the woods would become a safe area where students could play disc-golf and walk to school without being scared.

4. How was your project linked to the curriculum and how did it further academic achievement of students?

The students study politics and government in their seventh-grade social studies class. This project helps students see how everything they are learning is really applied in real-life. This project helped to make real-life connections for the students. It worked out great: we talked about something in social studies class about how everyone has a voice and then the students had the opportunity to go out into their community and apply everything they had learned to a real-life situation.

5. How did participants have the opportunity for reflection?
The students had the opportunity to take a field trip to the State Bar of Wisconsin, in Madison, Wisconsin. In Madison, the students presented their portfolios in a simulated legislative hearing, demonstrating their knowledge and understanding of how public policy is formulated. They presented in front of many different congressional men and women and even the State Superintendent of Public Instruction. Each student received a certificate for participating and as a class; we received a ribbon and a plaque for coming in fifth place in the state. After the trip, as a class, we discussed the project and it seemed to be an amazing experience for all the students who were involved.

6. What were the materials, money, and "connections" needed to complete this project?
This project was done completely in the classroom, outside the school (walking distance—woods) and the computer lab. The only money that was needed was money for our poster board and mailing the poster board to Madison. The students wrote for grants to help finance the construction of the disc-golf.

7. Upon reflection, what are some revisions you would make should you attempt this project again?
When I do this project again I would like to try to have all four of my classes involved. This year I piloted the program and only had one class participate. I am definitely recommending this project for other classrooms to try.

8. What were your key project successes?
The entire project was a success. The students were able to work together to identify a problem in the community; they studied a public policy and developed an action plan for implementing their policy. The students put all of their information together on a poster board and put together a three ring binder with all their information. They then presented in Madison where the students did a great job of presenting their information to the congressional men and women. Greendale Middle School received fifth place in the entire state for their hard work and accomplishments. The students were very proud of their hard work and efforts. They did a great job working together as a class (teamwork). They showed tremendous amounts of maturity and growth throughout this entire project.

9. What were your key project challenges?
A challenge that we found while working on this project was trying to find money to pay for our disc-golf course. The students researched many companies and found out that it would cost about $15,000 to construct a disc-golf course in the woods behind the school. The students then wrote for three different grants to try to help finance this project. At this time, we have not found out about the status of those grants. This challenge not once discouraged the students because they knew they did this entire project on their own. They

learned that they have a voice even though they are children and they can do anything when they put their minds together and work together.

10. What lessons have you learned about trying to implement service learning in your classroom?
I learned that service learning is an amazing way to help students make connections between school/curriculum and academic studies and real-life experiences. I also learned that service learning is a way to show our students that they have a voice and they can make things happen in their community even though they are students. This service-learning project started from a few students wanting to try something new and blossomed into an amazing learning experience for twenty-nine seventh graders at Greendale Middle School.

PARTNERING WITH STUDENTS IN ACTION RESEARCH

Next is an interview with Mary Whalen, a recent recipient of a 2010 Rowland Foundation fellowship, who teaches high school social studies at Twinfield Union School in Plainfield, Vermont.

1. Please tell me about your project (grade level, content area, time period, events).
I have been teaching service-learning thick and thin models for approximately fifteen years. I have always embedded service learning into civic engagement content. I spent two years developing an action research project model and support for students across the state through the governor's institute on education.

2. Why did you start doing service learning with your students?
Initially I began because it was an application of some of the ideas that I was teaching—sustainability; however, I discovered that I needed students to take control of the entire process and focus on the process instead of the outcome. If I was force-feeding the project and outcome, then it was my value system they were acting on and not theirs.

3. How do you incorporate learning goals and curriculum into your service-learning projects?
The action research course is embedded into our social studies curriculum—I think there are very few schools that provide this opportunity for students as a credit-bearing core curriculum class. Learning goals are tied to critical thinking skills, and civic engagement, etc.

4. What do you find most satisfying about doing service learning? What do you find most challenging?
I find most satisfying that the student work has meaning to them, addresses an injustice and provides voice. Most challenging is . . . personally, teaching one course in this way is a full time class . . . so I feel like it could always be even

deeper. I've also spent two years raising lots of money to fulfill one of the action plans so the pursuing grants activity has been huge for me.

5. What advice would you give to someone just starting out with service learning? What do you wish you knew when you started out?
I think my greatest successes could not have been possible if I did not have school administration support. I was given the freedom to think out of the box and ask my own questions. I do wish I had time to reflect more, and the reflection that I have done is responsible for my being at a place where I am asking new and more difficult and more pertinent questions.

For me, reflection and finding your own voice and being free to adjust when necessary is crucial. Service learning is a good match for me—in the way that I do it—I think teachers need to find their own way and their own style to make it personally sustaining.

6. What do you think teachers need most to be successful doing service learning with their students?
I think they have to love it and do it because it is how they function and see the hope and beauty in the world. A teacher once asked our faculty when I taught at Harwood, "Do you teach for a world that is or a world that you would like to see?" I always thought I taught for a world that I would like to see, but the action research work I am doing is truly engaging me in a world that is, and it is . . . good.

I don't think I would be as practical and invested in my kids and teaching if I thought the best that we could be was out of reach—service learning makes me invested in what is.

COMMUNITY PARTNERS AND A GIFTED PROGRAM

Here is an interview with Virginia Hamilton, teacher of fifth- and sixth-grade gifted students in Florida. She takes an unconventional approach with her teaching by using service learning to have students assist a local animal shelter.

1. Please tell me about your project (grade level, content area, time period, events).

- Grades 5 and 6, gifted and academically talented students
- Content areas are language arts, math, civic studies, music, art, computers
- 2002 to present
- Nine bus trips per month to South Animal Care Center in Melbourne and Central Brevard Humane Society in Cocoa, Florida.

2. Why did you start doing service learning with your students?
I first started Canine Commandos when service learning was a requirement for gifted students. I knew that if the project was going to be a continuation year

after year and be a success, I needed to find something that would interest the students. I was watching Animal Planet channel when an obedience trainer said that dogs are overlooked for adoption due to lack of training. He said that these dogs could be trained in minutes a day. What goes better together than peanut butter and jelly? Dogs and kids! It was a no-brainer. So with the support of administration, county, and parents, Canine Commandos was born. Everything Commando related has been student created.

3. How do you incorporate learning goals and curriculum into your service-learning projects?
I use Florida's Gifted Frameworks and Sunshine State Standards. I also applied for the Gifted Curriculum Challenge Grant and was awarded $10,000. This allowed a total of eleven schools to train. All schools work on different assignments to incorporate learning. Some projects include scrapbooking, school newspapers, bulletin board updates, Claymation video, Photo Stories, and writing a theme song.

4. What do you find most satisfying about doing service learning? What do you find most challenging?
I am such an animal activist including being a vegetarian. Animals give so much to human life; I cannot imagine not having pets in the house. The most satisfying part is knowing these kids are making a difference, helping find homes for the dogs. The most challenging is working with a dog that does not want to cooperate *and* trying to find enough time in each day for the students to work on their projects (these students are a weekly pull-out, one day per month).

5. What advice would you give to someone just starting out with service learning? What do you wish you knew when you started out?
The advice I would give would be to find something that you are passionate about. We all do food drives and it is necessary, but is it memorable? Find a project that is sustainable. Each year we add on a new project. Next year, we'd like to contact a university with film studies to do a documentary with us. What I wish I knew when we first started is what service learning really meant. It took a few years to get the hang of it and truly understand the difference between service learning and community service.

6. What do you think teachers need most to be successful doing service learning with their students?
Support! I receive several contacts from organizations and one of their concerns is lack of support by their school and/or district.

SUSTAINABILITY: CIVIC ENGAGEMENT IN HIGH SCHOOL

Jean Berthiume was Vermont's Teacher of the Year in 2009. He has developed many service-learning projects using various models with his high school students.

1. Please tell me about your teaching experience, content area, grade level, and the types of projects you are doing.

I've been teaching for fifteen years and started off in alternative education for the first two and for the last thirteen years I've been in the social studies/ history department at Harwood Union High School. I've taught most courses offered in the department and have settled on teaching a unique and progressive civics course entitled Creating Sustainable Communities, U.S. History, and a few electives such as psychology and current events. Grade level that I'm teaching now and have been for the last five years has been tenth through twelfth.

As for the types of projects I've done, I've done a wide variety of service-learning projects. To name a few:

- Vermont Stories of Modern America—U.S. History students studying modern American history spend time researching and learning the general narrative of events such as WWII, the Korean War, Vietnam, the Red Scare and McCarthy, the Space Race, Civil Rights Movement, etc. The service project came from student inquiry regarding the effect of these events that shaped our nation on Vermont. So the class decided to collect oral history, gather evidence and artifacts from historical societies, etc., to tell a new narrative of modern American history that was told through the portal of Vermont. Students found and collected riveting oral histories, artifacts, and photos that enabled them to create a video that was entitled "Vermont Stories of Modern America." Students made every decision about the video. Students collectively were consulted to edit the video, collected photos and short video clips to help tell the stories that they had collected, to deciding the music that best defined the era. In addition, the cover of the DVD was designed by students. Students even organized a premier for the film that celebrated the interviewees that shared their stories. A copy of the video was distributed to local historical societies, the Vermont Historical Society, and the Library of Congress.
- Kaleidoscope Project—The Kaleidoscope Project came out of my civics class entitled Creating Sustainable Communities. In a discrimination unit I was teaching, students were learning about power and privilege within society. Students spend time researching discrimination stories from the Holocaust to the story of Matthew Shepard (via the Laramie Project). We then all (including myself) wrote our own discrimination stories. Before sharing these stories, we discussed how we can safely share these stories with each other as a class. Students gave voice to what they needed from their peers and teacher before sharing these stories.

After spending three days or so on a list of agreements we all signed the sheet of paper that listed them. Students for the next week or so shared their stories and allowed for discussions to occur after each story. In the end a few students raised a comment/question for me and the class. The comment was, "Mr. B we get it now and understand how power and privilege is gained and acquired. How can we share with others the lessons and stories we just heard?" At that point I facilitated a discussion with the class about whether or not we could engage in a service-learning project that would make a difference within our community. Students discussed many different ideas about how they could share what they have learned and in doing so how they would further their own understanding about the problem facing our society.

A few students came back the next day and suggested that why can't we take some of our stories and work with graphic design students here at Harwood and share our stories. Another student spoke up and said, "Yeah . . . teachers are always buying posters that depict adolescents somewhere else, but what would happen if we used our own faces and stories?" So at that point the Kaleidoscope Project was born. Four stories were selected from the class and appropriate measures were taken to protect and safeguard the well-being of the student's whose stories were to be put on display in the halls of our school. Students surveyed the students before and a month after to see what effect these posters had on the school. Students were surprised to see that the posters positively changed the climate of our school. Other data was collected such as discipline referrals and there was a significant decrease in harassment or infractions relating to discrimination.

2. Why did you start doing service learning with your students?
I guess I've always done it, even before I even knew it was service learning.

These millennials are interested in social justice and being creative. I feel like when the audience is not just me for students that the quality of their work increases.

3. How do you incorporate learning goals and curriculum into your service-learning projects?
I use a couple of tools; one is UbD (Understanding by Design) and secondly, the KIDS consortium's KIDS Framework for high-quality service learning.

4. What do you find most satisfying about doing service learning? What do you find most challenging?
What I find most satisfying about doing service learning is the opportunity to make learning relevant, real, and rigorous for my students. Students learn best when they can discover themselves in what they are learning.

What is most challenging is that service learning is not always a linear path! :)

5. What do you wish you knew when you started out?
My advice to someone just starting out . . . start small and help your students connect what they are learning to the world around them. Allow your students to discover authentic needs with your school or greater community. Give students an opportunity to make sense of a situation, need within the community, or how to see a problem from multiple perspectives.

6. What do you think teachers need most to successfully do service learning with their students?

Teachers need to have good facilitation skills and a good understanding of ethnography so that teachers don't fall into the trap of simply doing community service.

PROJECT-BASED LEARNING: EXTREME WEATHER

Courtney Elliot is a fourth- and fifth-grade teacher at Proctor Elementary School in Proctor, Vermont. I had the good fortune of working with her to develop project-based learning in her classroom. Proctor Elementary is a partner school with the Tarrant Institute of Innovative Education, where I work as a professional development coordinator.

1. Please tell me about your project (grade level, content area, time period, events).
For my first PBL [project-based learning] project my fourth- and fifth-grade combination class worked on extreme weather. We started with what is climate and what is weather. Then we moved onto climate zones and how each one has different weather patterns that the states within it typically follow. After that we did work on what causes different types of extreme weather and how do meteorologists know when to issue alerts to the public. After a field trip to WCAX we talked about risk assessments in different climate zones and then covered disaster relief efforts. The unit took about three months to complete with all the scaffolding of what is PBL and the team roles and cumulated in four teams creating a script and newscaster revolving around a topic of their choice that related to extreme weather.

2. Why did you start doing project based learning with your students?
I originally started PBL with my students after my school partnered with the Tarrant Institute of Innovative Education for professional development.

3. How do you incorporate learning goals and curriculum into project-based learning?
My biggest concern was being able to make sure that I was hitting my standards within my PBL and I found out that PBL lends itself nicely to not only my weather content but to transferable skills such as teamwork, problem solving, and active listening. During the course of the unit the students were asked to work in teams, partners, and individually. They wrote mini research reports on disasters, explored domain specific vocabulary, read nonfiction books and articles at the 4/5 level, actively reported to the group and listened to others, created a project visual, such as a hurricane proof house or a first aid kit, drafted and revised a script, and used technology to film and edit their own newscast video in the classroom.

4. What do you find most satisfying about doing PBL? What do you find most challenging?
The most satisfying part of PBL for me as an educator was seeing how well my students could adapt and problem solve on their own. Many teams sur-

prised me so much in their final videos. They took what they had learned and researched and created scripts that really informed their target audience. They worked to follow a planner and set time goals for finishing projects which they met as fourth- and fifth-graders. They did all their work in the classroom and came to me for help when needed. They were engaged and worked towards fostering academic independent. The most challenging part of PBL for me as an educator was helping groups to problem solve team conflicts. Many groups worked very hard at this skill on their own. I found I had one group that constantly needed a referee up until the final days of the project. It was challenging to help this group work cohesively while making sure the very different needs of the other three groups were met.

5. What advice would you give to someone just starting out with PBL? What do you wish you knew when you started out?
If I had to give out advice on starting PBL I would say to scaffold and take your first one slowly. I originally had these plans to just throw my class right into the PBL fire but even at fourth- and fifth-grade level the skill set wasn't there yet. I think what really helped my class was the scaffolding. We introduced one team role at a time and had a chance to practice it for a week in a mini-project format. This also gave my students chances to work different people and allow me to see what team combinations would work well in the big project. I scaffolded student choice as well. I made sure they had a voice but were directed in an effective direction. Something I wish I knew would be how long it would take so I could have started a little earlier than I did.

6. What do you think teachers need most to be successful doing PBL with their students?
I think to be successful with PBL teachers need an open mind. They need to realize that the kids won't sink being given choice and freedom if it is done in an effective and structured way. The students will rise to meet your expectations when given the room to do so in their own ways.

7. What impact has PBL had on your students, school, and/or community?
I think the biggest impact PBL has had on my students is that it has made them more eager to learn. They feel that they are the teachers and they have control over what information is important to be taught to someone else. It really encouraged critical thinking for my students.

These are just a few examples of teachers who are currently using service learning in their classrooms with great success. Take the little gems from them: resources, inspiration, ideas for projects, and tips for how to begin. Then begin your own story. What problem will your class help to solve? Where will their interest, motivation and ideas take your students? How will you help shape our future leaders, by letting them begin to do the real work that is required in a democracy—research, problem solving, communication, and action? The answer is up to you. My hope is now after reading this book the task is less daunting, and more exciting and invigorating to your teaching. Let your students change the world, and get ready to show everyone what they have done.

Afterword

It's not always easy to do the right thing in education. As teachers, we know the best ways to teach and reach our students. But with many of the conditions in today's classrooms—chopped-up schedules, standardized testing environments, pressure from parents and administrators, and behavior challenges—it is easier to just do the same kind of teaching many of us had as children (lectures and note taking). Or teach the same units we've been teaching for years. We know the value of project- and inquiry-based learning, but the realities of making it happen are much easier said than done.

For today's children, though, service learning, PBL, and other forms of innovative teaching should be the norm, not the exception. With society's ever-increasing challenges and rapid and instant changes to technology and the way we communicate, we need to be raising critical-thinking, problem-solving, community-minded citizens.

Service and project-based learning is one way you can do just that. You might have to fit it in creatively; you might have to integrate it with what you already teach (as described in this book). By doing so, you are honoring what is better for our students, academically, socially, and for the world.

I frequently tell my students not to always take the easy road. For you as a teacher, I encourage the same. Service and project-based learning is not easy, but I hope this book has made it more doable and manageable for you. As you proceed with service learning and PBL, you will learn invaluable lessons that you can then pass on to other interested teachers. When that happens, teacher by teacher, student by student, we are changing the world.

Appendices

Principal Discussion Guide

Use this to convince your principal to support your work in service learning. This can also be easily modified and copied for use with parents.
  Service Learning:

- Raises standardized test scores.
- Improves attendance
- Develops a sense of civic responsibility
- Improves GPA
- Develops critical thinking skills
- Improves student behavior and positive attitudes
- Promotes a strong school and community connection
- Allows for more parent volunteerism and involvement
- Solves school and community problems
- Is innovative, creative and integrated learning
- Promotes twenty-first-century learning skills

Project Based Learning

- Can increase retention of content
- Improve students' attitudes towards learning

For full citations, please see the reference section at the end of this book.

APPENDIX 3.0

Service Learning Project Idea List (by academic subject)

Teachers: Keep in mind this is a list of service learning ideas, and not a laundry list of community service projects. To be service learning, it needs to be integrated into your curricular goals, and provide for assessment and reflection of learning. These are just a few ideas per topic. You're sure to think of more, and you'll find more ideas sprinkled throughout this book.

These ideas can be adapted to any grade level.

Science (including health)

- Lake, pond, river or stream assessment and action (clean-up, legislation, park development, preservation of habitat, invasive species removal, bio-diversity study, species assessment, species study and conservation, etc.).
- Local habitat preservation (teams assess, sign, and teach about a local habitat). This could be any habitat.
- Local species preservation (teams discover local species in need, work to protect them and teach others). This could be any species.
- A disease or condition of the human body present in the local community (students learn about it, interview health care providers and experts, then teach the school community about it).
- Local geological areas of interest (learn about the area's geologic history, develop a community resource, and teach about it).
- Study how robotics are used in our society, such as to aid construction, people with disabilities, or in industry- create a prototype of similar de-sign, and share with the school community.
- Human body tests to promote fitness (students could develop health and fitness tests for the school community, then communicate results and how to improve for better fitness).
- Create a picture book about a science theme. Share this with a younger grade level.

Language Arts, English or Literacy

- Interview local authors, create a community resource, and share it with the school community.
- Interview community elders, create a community resource or project, and share it with the school community.
- Create films about your school's literacy program. Edit and finalize, then share with the school community.
- Create plays in the style of a studied author or within a theme. Perform for the school.

- Create a newspaper or magazine for your community, with all the parts. Find community funding and share.

Math

- Hold a math night for the community. Students plan all the details within a curricular theme.
- Create a picture book about math themes and concepts to share with the younger grades.
- Interest younger grades in math. Hold a math fair and develop high interest activities to lead.
- Interview local professionals who use math in their jobs. Create a community resource (book, website, guide) and share.
- Develop a web quest or online tutorial for a math concept or concepts to share.
- Create a series of math games (in a curricular area assigned) for your grade level and share.
- Create how-to math videos to post on YouTube or share with younger grades.

Social Studies

- Develop a play, book, video, or website to communicate a period of time and share with the community.
- Create a song, poem, or puppet show to teach about an historical figure, important event, or time period. Post on a blog or website.
- Hold a history fair within a curricular theme. Students study their historical person fully, dress up in character, and talk with the school community at the fair.
- Create new legislation to solve a community problem. Take it to a local legislator, or the capitol of your state to share.
- Interview local politicians about a topic tied to your curricular goals. Create a way to share these interviews (movie, website, play, poem, newspaper, etc.).

Music

- Create musical instruments from reused and recycled materials. Teach the younger grades about how to play them, then donate them to a class.
- Create a musical score to describe something: a season, a feeling, or a curricular theme. Then share with the school or world on YouTube!

- Interview local musicians about a theme or curricular goal in music. Then share with the school community what you have learned.
- Write songs to share about a theme in music class. Share with the school (or wider) community.

Art

- Find a community need for art: a mural in an alley, hospital or clinic, run down area of down, on the side of the school, and work together to create it.
- Find someone in the community in need. Create art for that person based on their interests and present it to them in a community event.
- For an agreed upon charity, create an art show. Create art to sell in an evening community event to fundraise for the charity (or your school).
- Teach the younger grades about an art concepts, famous artist, or period of time in art. Discover a creative way to teach them about it.

Physical Education

- Interview the staff of a school about their exercise habits. Create a movie, book or website to share with the school community.
- Hold a school wide fitness or wellness event. Students plan and coordinate the whole event with teacher support.

APPENDIX 3.1

Dear Parents and Guardians,

I am currently planning an exciting new multidisciplinary unit of study. The (NGSS, or district standards, or proficiencies) calls for the sciences to be connected and integrated. This unit will do just that. Our focus will be on the natural and cultural history of the Worcester Mountain Range and its watershed.

Our approach will be through Service Learning. Service Learning is a "method of teaching and learning that challenges students to identify research, propose, and implement solutions to real needs in their school or community" (KIDS Consortium, 2001). Service learning is an approach to teaching and learning that has been linked to increased engagement and personal growth in students.

Our unit on the Worcester Mountain Watershed will utilize resources in our own community. Student research will add to our community's awareness of our local natural resources.

With clear teacher guidance, Service Learning allows students to drive the course of study and action. I will provide instruction, along with community volunteers and experts, as well as resources and connections to facilitate projects that students select. Students will have a Celebrate the Worcester Watershed Community Day where they share their work with the school and greater community. Specific science instruction during this unit may take the form of aquatic and or forest ecology, as well as other sciences. Additionally, student groups may branch into other ideas. There will be a portfolio for assessment that students will complete, with expectations clearly outlined. I will share a copy of this portfolio for you to look at with your child. Please also see the attached standards that will be addressed by this unit.

Please consider volunteering to help us with this project. Any time you can give would be helpful, and I have many ideas for ways that you can support our work. Please call or email me, or send in a note of interest with your child, and I will get back to you with specific ways that you can volunteer.

Please feel free to call with questions or concerns. I feel this is an exciting opportunity for our fifth and sixth grade students, and I hope you do too!

Sincerely,

Katy Farber, 5/6 Teacher, Rumney School

5/6 Wonders of the Worcester Watershed Unit

Standards Linking

Students in our 5/6 unit will have the opportunity to meet several of the Vermont Standards throughout their study. Some standards will be focused on more than others as a result of the topic of study. Listed below are the standards I believe will be met throughout this unit.

Transferrable Skills are personal development standards that cut across all field of knowledge. This unit will involve students working on their projects in small groups, which will provide many opportunities for growth in the area of the Vital Results.

The areas of the Transferrable Skills that this unit will address are: Communication, Reasoning and Problem Solving, Personal Development and Civic/Social Responsibility.

Communication: Students will need to research their topic idea using technology, reading in content areas, listening to presentations, writing for an authentic purpose, and using presentation skills.

Reasoning and Problem Solving: Students will ask guiding questions, select a focus, and think creatively.

Personal Development: Students will have choices in this project, which will help them develop a sense of personal competence. They will have to make informed, educated decisions and work collaboratively within a student team.

Civic/Social Responsibility: Students will gain an understanding of community values and democratic processes, and learn by serving our Middlesex community information about the Worcester Mountain watershed area.

Fields of Knowledge

Geography

Geographical Knowledge

Standard 6.7 Students use geographical knowledge and images of various places to understand the present, communicate historical interpretations, develop solutions for problems, and plan for the future.

Curricular goal: Students in this unit will use mapping skills, strive to learn the physical and cultural geography of our area, analyze land-use problems, and research how geography influences our communities.

Interrelationships

Standard 6.9 Students examine the interrelationships among physical earth processes, ecosystems and human activities.

Curricular goal: Students in this unit will locate and describe various ecosystems in Vermont, demonstrate how human actions can modify the environment, and will examine the interrelationships between earth's ecosystems.

Inquiry, Experimentation and Theory

Scientific Method

Standard 7.1 Students use scientific methods to describe, investigate, and explain phenomena.

Curricular goal: Students in this unit may chose to design an experiment, which uses the scientific method.

Standard 7.2 Students design and conduct a variety of their own investigations and projects.

Curricular goal: Students in this service learning project will be designing and conducting their own research project and presentation.

Systems

Analysis

Standard 7.11 Students analyze and understand living and non-living systems as collections of interrelated parts and interconnected systems.

Curricular goal: Students will demonstrate throughout this unit an understanding that systems are connected and how one effects how others work.

> **The Living World**
> Organisms, Evolution and Interdependence
> Standard 7.13 Students understand the characteristics of organisms, see patterns of similarity and differences among living organisms, understand the role of evolution, and recognize the interdependence of all systems that support life.
> Curricular goal: Students in this unit will investigate the interdependence of all systems that support life (water cycle, food chains, populations).

APPENDIX 3.2

Bloom's Thinking Taxonomy (1956)

Level 1
  Knowledge-Recall
  Verbs: tell, list, describe, name, locate
  Level 2
  Comprehension-Understanding
  Verbs: restate, outline, predict
  Level 3
  Application-Transfer
  Verbs: show, solve, use, illustrate, examine, classify
  Level 4
  Analysis-Examining
  Verbs: analyze, investigate, compare and contrast, distinguish
  Level 5
  Synthesis-Combining
  Verbs: create, invent, construct, design, compose, plan, imagine
  Level 6
  Evaluation-Rating
  Verbs: judge, select, choose, debate, justify, recommend, assess

APPENDIX 3.3

Wonders of the Worcester Watershed Guiding Questions

Background information: Our school sits in the Worcester Mountain Range. We see the mountains outside of our school everyday. Many of your homes are in and around the mountains. What is a watershed? Many of you studied this concept in science last year. A watershed is land area from which a river and all its tributaries get their water (also called a drainage basin).

During this brainstorm you will think about what you want to know about this unique community in which we live. During this unit, as we discussed in the introduction, you will get to research a subject you are interested in, and create some way to share your information with the Middlesex community.

To help you get started in generating ideas, take a look at some of the materials set out in your classroom. There are some books, maps and pictures to help you.

Then independently answer the following questions. After that, you'll share with a small group, then with the whole class. This will help us understand your areas of interest.

1. What do you want to investigate about our local mountains and watershed?

2. What do you recommend or imagine Middlesex community members should know about the Worcester mountains and watershed?

3. What are you curious about in our area? What have you always wanted to learn more about but have never had the chance? Create a question (or 2 or 3) about anything you would like to learn more about within our local mountains and watershed. (Please write your answers in a question format.)

APPENDIX 3.4

Wonders of the Worcester Watershed
  Master Question List
  Directions: These are all of the student response to the guided questions. Read through the questions below. They are broken into areas of interest. Please number your preference for a project topic from one to five (one being your first choice, through five). Put the number clearly to the right of the chosen question. Thanks!
  WW=Worcester Watershed
  Physical Science
  1. What are the water sources of the WW and why is it called that?
  2. How did the WW form?
  3. Where does the most water flow in the WW and where does it start and end?
  4. What and where are the different tributaries (streams and rivers) coming off of Hunger Mountain?
  5. How does the WW work?
  6. Why is the top of Hunger Mountain bald?
  7. How has the mountain environment changed over the years?
  8. How has the weather effected the WW over time and have there been any major storms in history?
  9. Has Vermont ever had an earthquake? When, where and why?
  10. What would a map or model of the entire WW look like?
  11. What is the geological history of the WW?
  12. Have there been fires or floods in the WW? If so, when and what were the effects?
  13. What mapping skills would help you travel on foot in the WW?
  14. What soil type is found in the WW and what can be learned about it?
  15. What mountains and communities make up the WW?
  Life Science
  1. Are there still wolves in Vermont? What is the history of sightings and predictions?
  2. What is the most common animal in the WW and what can be learned about it?
  3. What is the history of bears in the WW?
  4. Why are there so many fishers?
  5. What animals were here in history that aren't anymore? What happened and why?
  6. What reptiles live and how do they develop?
  7. Are there any endangered species that live in the WW? What are they and what is there status?

8. What plants are dangerous that live here?

9. What hawks live in the WW and what can I learn about them?

10. What lives in the swamps, marshes and wetlands and where are they located in the WWW?

11. What turtles live in the WW and how do they sound, eat and function?

12. Are bobcats going extinct? What can be learned about there current population?

13. When was the last mountain lion seen and are there any left?

14. What kind of buys live in the WW?

15. Where do frogs live in the WW? What kinds are here? What do they eat? How do roads affect them?

16. What animal habitats are in the WW?

17. What tracks go with what animal? What can they tell us?

18. What fish live in ponds, rivers and streams in the WW?

19. What is the biology of raccoons?

Social

1. What are the legends, history and stories of the WW?

2. Who were some of the first people here?

3. Who discovered Hunger Mountain? What was their story?

4. How long has Hunger Mountain been named and was it called something else at one point?

5. Have people in the past ever lived on Hunger Mountain?

6. Why are there stone walls in the woods? What can we learn from them?

7. What is the highest population of the WW and what are the impacts on our area?

8. What plants are/were used to cure illnesses?

9. What do you do if you run into a wild animal?

10. What minerals can be found in the WW? Is there any gold?

11. What are good wilderness skills for surviving in the mountains?

Human Impact

1. How does pollution travel and affect the WW?

2. How do we decide what a good use of our land is in the WW?

3. How do humans affect the ecosystems of WW?

4. What does it mean to be an ethical hunter?

5. How "clean" is our water?

6. What trails are in this area, and where are they accessed?

7. Is there pollution in our rivers and how is it affecting the WW?

8. Is global warming affecting our snow totals? What can be learned about this?

APPENDIX 4.1

Planning Checklist (these concepts are outlined more fully in chapter 4)

- decide on the length of the unit
- schedule the culminating event (learning fair or festival)
- meet with your teaching team
- meet with your principal
- share about your project with the school staff
- plan your assessments for the unit
- brainstorm your needed resources
- get organized (binder or system for all the project materials)
- plan for the culminating event (where, when, who will be invited, publicize)
- plan for pre-teaching

APPENDIX 4.2

PBL Planning Template

PBL Planning Template
   by Katy Farber, Ed.D
   Tarrant Institute for Innovative Education, UVM
   Created from resources at Edutopia, Buck Institute and others

Project Name_____

Grade Level_____

Project Area_____

Team Teachers_____

1. Decide what content proficiencies/performance indicators you hope to address with the project. List these below. Can be integrated across subjects. Also consider the transferrable skills.

1. Decide on a guiding question you would like students to consider. It should create interest and a feeling of challenge. Examples:

- What is epic poetry?
- How have native peoples been impacted by changes in the world?
- How does probability relate to games?
- Why is science important and how can it help save people?

Guiding Question

1. Decide on an authentic project idea or several ideas for students to pick from. Or let students generate these ideas (books, videos, maps, websites, models, plays).

Describe the project.

4. Decide on a community sharing event. Make it authentic and important. Consider inviting parents, the community, the school board, and interested community organizations.

Describe the community sharing event (also called culminating event)

5. Schedule the event and work backwards to create a timeline for the project.

Rough timeline (list important dates)

6. What scaffolding or supports might be needed? List websites, readings, resources, and job roles that you think would work for your students.

Scaffolding

7. Design reflection opportunities. Students should be reflecting throughout the experience. What might this look like (weekly journals, blogs, illustrations)?

Reflection

8. Design assessments. These can be teamwork oriented, product oriented, and content oriented, or all three! See examples in the resources.

Assessments-- modify, create or link rubrics here

APPENDIX 5.1

Contact Log:
    Students, teachers and parents: enter in the names, jobs and contact information for everyone you contact regarding the project.

Person contacting	Role or job	Type of contact (email, call, interview, letter)	date

APPENDIX 5.2

Parent Survey

Dear Parents and Guardians,

Please take a moment to tell me a little about your profession, interests, hobbies, and your potential interest in volunteering in your child's classroom. It is very important for children to be exposed to as many role models as possible, and your involvement over the next year would enrich our studies and connection to the community. Thanks for your time!

Name_____

Job:_____

Hobbies:_____

Sports interests:_____

Special skills and interests: _____

Would you be willing to share about any of the above topics with our class? _____

Would you be willing to do a presentation about your job?

_____

Would you be willing to volunteer to help with our service learning projects?

_____

Please list any other way you might be involved in volunteering this year (field trip chaperone, student assistance, room parent and organizer, or any other ideas!)

_____

Thank you.

APPENDIX 5.3

Sample Press Release

Headline Is in Title Case Meaning You Capitalize Every Word Except for Prepositions and Articles of Three Words or Less and Short; Ideally it is Not More Than 170 Characters and Does Not Take a Period

The summary paragraph is a synopsis of the press release in regular sentence form. It doesn't merely repeat the headline or opening paragraph. It just tells the story in a different way. The summary paragraph is mandatory at Free Press Release Center.

City, State (FPRC) Month 1, 2005—The first paragraph know as the "lead" contains the most important information. You need to grab your reader's attention here. And you can't assume that they have read the headline or summary paragraph; the lead should stand on its own.

A press release, like a news story, keeps sentences and paragraphs short, about three or four lines per paragraph. The first couple of paragraphs should cover the who, what, when, where, why and how questions.

The rest of the news release expounds on the information provided in the lead paragraph. It includes quotes from key staff, customers or subject matter experts. It contains more details about the news you have to tell, which can be about something unique or controversial or about a prominent person, place or thing.

"You should include a quote for that human touch," said Gary Sims, CEO of the Free Press Release Center. "And you should use the last paragraph to restate and summarize the key points."

This is a sample press release template for use at the Free Press Release Center. The last paragraph can also include details on product availability, trademark acknowledgements, etc.

About ABC Company:

Include a short corporate backgrounder about the company or the person who is newsworthy before you list the contact person's name and phone number.

Contact:

Name

Title

phone number

email/or web address

(Free Press Release Center, n.d.)

APPENDIX 5.4

Press Release Sample

MATH ROCKS! STUDENTS GIVE MATH AN IMAGE MAKEOVER

Math is underrated and often students who like it are stereotyped, and the students of Centre Hall School are taking this message to the community. Ms. Bevin's 7 th grade math classes have been creating a math fair to showcase how cool math can be. In groups of 3 or 4 students, these students have created projects to showcase their math skills and lift the profile of this subject.

State College, Pennsylvania, May 23, 2010—At Centre Hall School, students in the seventh grade took over the gym to showcase their cool math skills. As part of a service learning project led by 7th grade math teacher, Ms. Bevin, students set up stations and demonstrated their math skills to the entire middle school community. At one station, students lined up to take free throw shots at the basketball hoop, and students taught each other how to calculate their own sports stats, using fractions, decimals and percents. At another station, tessellation art was hung on the walls and students showed small groups how to create them. This project is part of a school wide effort to make math come alive for students and to connect it to real life.

Ms. Bevin was clearly proud of her students. She said, "Math doesn't have to be sedentary or boring. These students are making it come alive for every-one—and showing each other that they can enjoy learning and teaching math. "

Principal Phil Bosco agreed. " I grew up doing math alone, at my desk, in isolation. I didn't enjoy it very much. I wish I had Ms. Bevin back in 7th grade. I think this kind of hands on learning will empower some of our students to see themselves as mathematicians—and possibly have a future in this area."

About Ms. Bevins:
   Ms. Bevins is in her 4th year teaching at Centre Hall School and believes service learning projects like this motivate and inspire her students.

Contact:
   Ms. Bevins, 7th Grade Math Teacher at Centre Hall School
   888-888-8888

APPENDIX 7.1

Name_____

Students: Please make sure all the items listed below are present and in this order. Check when completed. The blank lines at the end of the list are for you to include different assessments particular to your project.
   Table of Contents
   _____ brainstorming web
   _____ planning sheet
   _____ timeline
   _____ content area reading
   _____ 5 journal entries (dated)
   _____ project notes and information
   _____ vocabulary list
   _____ supporting questions
   _____ presentation notes
   _____ research/information
   _____ diagrams, drawings and charts

_____ self assessments
_____ weekly self-assessments
_____ weekly group assessments
_____ unit teamwork rubric
_____ project rubric

_____ _____

_____ _____

APPENDIX 7.2

Brainstorming Web

Student Directions: Put your guiding question or topic in the center. List any and all ideas about what to do for your service learning project. Remember to include written and visual ways to share information, and be creative!

Project Title:

Appendices

APPENDIX 7.3

Timeline for Service Learning Project

Person	Task (job)	Due date	notes	Check when complete

Overall Project Due Date:_____
Service Learning Festival:_____

APPENDIX 7.4

Student Planning Sheet- Service Learning Project

Focus Question or Topic Area:

Directions: Please describe the project you plan on completing with your group. It needs to have visual and written components. See the project rubric for the requirements. These can be combined into one project, but the parts need to be handed in and complete.

Visual (a way of communicating your information visually to the audience):

Written (script, report, story, and so on communicating information about your topic area):

Materials you think you will need:

How will your project help the community?

APPENDIX 7.5

Content Area Reading

Directions: When you get a source that has information, from the internet, a book, magazine, or newspaper, be sure to write down the information here to keep track of your work. Try to have at least 5 different sources with variety.

Type of Source	Title	Author	Page numbers or internet site address

APPENDIX 7.6

Vocabulary List

Directions: Write down new vocabulary that you learn in your research. You will be expected to list and define at least ten words and thoroughly understand their meaning.

word	meaning

APPENDIX 7.7

Supporting Questions:

Directions: As you come up with more detailed and focused questions during your research, please write them down on this sheet. Put a check next to questions your group is able to answer during this project. You can show your answers in several ways—in your project's written or visual component, or orally during the presentation. Have a goal of ten questions (with at least eight answered!)

Question	Answered?

APPENDIX 7.8

Service Learning Project Rubric

	1 (limited work shared)	2 (does not meet standards)	3 (close to meeting standards)	4 (meeting the standard)
Visual	Limited visual presented	Visual is partially completed, or not very clear, colorful or detailed, communicated some learned information, but it is not organized.	Visual is complete showing detail, color and clear information; some aspect of the visual has problem(s) with clarity and/or understanding	Visual is complete, organized, clear and detailed, communicates learned information in a creative and understandable way.
Written	Limited written piece shared	Partially complete, lacks details or focus, or is in rough draft form with errors; communicates some information learned in research process	Complete in final draft form and shows an understanding of the information learned in the research process, some problems with the piece are evident	Complete in final draft form and shows a thorough understanding of the information learned in the research process, is interesting and engaging to the reader
Presentation	Student did not have a role in the presentation	Student had a limited role in the presentation	Student had a role in the presentation, used some good speaking skills, and shared information	Student had well-rehearsed role in the presentation; used good speaking skills and shared information enthusiastically with the school community

** To achieve a 5, a student needs to show exceptional effort in the visual, written and presentation portions of this project. This will be clearly evident from the quality in each area. Extending the project beyond standards can include more depth of study, a creative and unique approach to the project's written and visual, and an outstanding and creative presentation.

Updated Service Learning Scale for new edition

Service/Project Based Learning Project Rubric
(visual, written, presentation, and technology)
Updated using Vermont's Transferrable Skills and Proficiencies

Learning Target	Getting Started	Making Progress	Proficient	Proficient with Distinction
Demonstrate effective, expressive, and receptive communication including oral, written, multimedia, and performance. **Proficiency:** Clear and Effective Communication	I can design or sketch a **visual component** that shows some understanding of my topic.	I can edit and sketch a colorful or detailed **visual element** of the project with some new information.	I can complete **visual elements** of the project showing detail, color and clear information about my topic.	I can create an organized, clear and detailed **visual elements** that communicate learned information in a creative and understandable way.
Demonstrate effective, expressive, and receptive communication including oral, written, multimedia, and performance. **Proficiency:** Clear and Effective Communication	I can share ideas about information learned in the research process.	I can partially complete **written components** that share some information learned in research process	I can create **written components** in final draft form that shows an understanding of the information learned in the research process.	I can create **written components** in final draft form and show a thorough understanding of the information learned in the research process, in a way that is interesting and engaging to the reader.
Demonstrate effective, expressive, and receptive communication including oral, written, multimedia, and performance. **Proficiency:** Clear and Effective Communication	I can plan having a role in **presenting**.	I can start having a role in the **presentation**.	I can have a role in the **presentation**; use some speaking skills, and shared information.	I can **present** well-rehearsed role in the presentation; use speaking skills and share information with enthusiasm with the school community.
Use technology to further enhance and disseminate communication **Proficiency:** Clear and Effective Communication	I am starting to use **technology**, or planning on how to use it, to share information in my project.	I can begin to use **technology** to share information learned in my project.	I can use **technology** to share information learned in my project.	I can use **technology** creatively to share information learned in my project.

** Specific content learning targets can be added to this based on the subject area and learning goals**

APPENDIX 7.9

Weekly Journal

Teachers: Assign a specific length based on the age of the students you work with.

Name_____

Directions: During the unit, please reflect weekly about your project. You can write about lots of thoughts about your service learning project. Some ideas:

- What you have learned and connections to your new knowledge
- Describe your experiences with your group as you discover new information
- Describe a hands-on experience within this project
- Explain what this project makes you think about
- Your concerns, thoughts and ideas about how to solve a problem you discovered
- Describe your feelings about your group, topic area, or the project in general

APPENDIX 7.10

Teamwork Rubric: Student self assesses in pencil, hands it in, and the teacher assesses in pen.

	1 (limited teamwork demonstrated)	2 (does not meet standards)	3 (close to meeting standards)	4 (meets the standard)	5 (exceeds the standard)
Research and Gather Information	Does not collect any information that relates to the topic	Collects very little information- some relates to the topic	Collects some basic information- most relates to the topic	Collects a great deal of information— all relates to the topic	Collects a great deal of information—all relates to the topic—helps other in the research process
Share Information	Does not relay any information to teammates	Relays very little information- some relates to the topic	Relays some basic information- most relates to the topic	Relays a great deal of information- all relates to the topic	Relays a great deal of information- goes beyond what is expected
Be Punctual	Does not hand in any assignments	Hands in most assignments late	Hands in assignments some of the time	Hands in assignments most of the time	Hands in all assignments on time
Fulfill Team Duties	Does not perform any duties of assigned team role	Performs very little duties	Performs nearly all duties	Performs all duties of assigned team role	Performs all duties assigned team role- and goes above and beyond that role
Share Equally	Always relies on others to do the work	Rarely does the assigned work— often needs reminding	Usually does the assigned work- sometimes needs reminding	Does the assigned work with very little reminding	Always does the assigned work without having to be reminded

Updated Teamwork Rubric

	Getting Started	Making Progress	Proficient	Proficient with Distinction
Research and Gather Information	Collects information- some that relates to the topic	Collects some basic information- most relates to the topic	Collects a great deal of information— all relates to the topic	Collects a great deal of information—all relates to the topic—helps other in the research process
Share Information	Relays some information- some relates to the topic	Relays some basic information- most relates to the topic	Relays a great deal of information- all relates to the topic	Relays a great deal of information- goes beyond what is expected
Be Punctual	Does some of the assignments of group work	Hands in some assignments on time to the group	Hands in most assignments of group work	Hands in all assignments on time
Fulfill Team Duties	Performs one or two team duties	Performs some team duties	Performs nearly all duties	Performs all duties assigned team role- and goes above and beyond that role
Share Equally	With guidance can start working on team tasks	Works on some team tasks with some reminders and support	Works on team tasks with little reminding	Works on team tasks and helps others

APPENDIX 7.11

Weekly Self Assessment

Students: Complete the self-assessment assignment every week during the project.

Name_____

Directions: Please answer the following questions in at least 2 sentences each.

1. How was my participation and motivation this week in my group?

2. What did I do well this week and what were some of my challenges?

3. What can I do next week to improve?

Weekly Group Assessment

Students: All students complete this weekly Group Assessment every week of the project. Do this independently.

1. How did my group members do with participation and motivation this week?

2. What were some of the things my group did well and what were some of the challenges?

3. What can my group do next week to improve?

APPENDIX 8.1

Small Group Reflection Questions:

- How is this group working together?
- What has been challenging?
- What has been going well, and why do you think that is?
- What has changed from your original plan?
- What has surprised you about your work?

- What questions has your work made you think of?
- How does your project connect with others?
- How can your group work more effectively with each other?
- What skills have you been using? What ones would you like to use?

APPENDIX 8.2

Whole Class Reflection Questions:

- Have each group share about their projects and work.
- Have students do a whip around (each class member shares briefly) about one interesting fact from their research.
- Ask students to say what has surprised them.
- Ask students what skills they have been using in their work, and how they could improve or expand them.
- Ask students to make connects to projects and other areas in academics or in life.
- Ask students if they could wave a magic wand and change something, what would it be?

APPENDIX 8.3

Journal Prompts:

- Describe your work today on your service-learning project.
- What was surprising? What changed your perspective?
- Describe how you were showing teamwork skills (or not).
- Describe how your teammates were using teamwork skills.
- Describe one piece of information you found particularly helpful, shocking, or interesting.
- Draw and label a diagram that reflects your new learning.
- Make a connection about your work, research and project to current events, academics, or your personal life.
- Draw or write a snapshot. If I were to take a picture of your group today, what would it look like?
- Describe what it is like to contact members of your community. Were you nervous? What did you gain from this?
- Describe one thing you could do to help your team work together better.

APPENDIX 8.4

Big Ideas and Questions:

Directions for Students—As you complete your research and work on your project, list any questions here that you think of that you want to know the answer to. Think big! It doesn't have to relate to your topic. It is wide open, just like your mind.

Questions:

1.
2.
3.
4.
5.
6.
7.
8.

These questions might lead you to some big ideas about the world. What do you think should happen next? What would you do if you could? How should the world change? What difference do you want to make?

1.
2.
3.
4.
5.

References

Association for Middle School Education. (2010). This we believe: 16 characteristics of successful schools. Retrieved from http://www.amle.org/AboutAMLE/ThisWeBelieve.aspx - 122516-the-16-characteristics.

Billig, S. H. (2004). Heads, hearts, and hands: The research on K-12 service-learning. In National Youth Leadership Council. *Growing to Greatness. The State of Service-Learning Report*, 12-25. St. Paul, MN: National Youth Leadership Council.

Billig, S. (2002). Using Evidence to Make the Case for Service-Learning as an Academic Achievement Intervention in K-12 Schools. Retrieved March 29, 2010 from http://www.seanetonline.org/images/UsingEvidencetoMaketheCaseforService.doc

Billig, S. (n.d.). Using Evidence to Make the Case for Service-Learning as an Academic Achievement Intervention in K-12 Schools. RMC Research Corporation. Retrieved March 20, 2010 from http://74.125.93.132/search?q=cache:Y6rUlJ41wj0J:www.service-learningpartnership.org/site/DocServer/caseforsl.doc%3FdocID%3D106+www.seanetonline.org/images/UsingEvidencetoMaketheCaseforService.doc+service+learning+and+standardized+testing&cd=1&hl=en&ct=clnk&gl=us.

Bishop, P. (2014). *The problem with genius hour.* Tarrant Institute for Innovative Education. Retrieved from http://tiie.w3.uvm.edu/blog/partner-with-students-in-a-Makerspace/

Brenner, J. (2010). Observations on Effective Teams: "Working Together Works" Concurrent Session Team Development & Tuckman's Model - In Brief. Retrieved July 19, 2010 at http://billasbi.weebly.com/uploads/4/4/7/7/4477114/tuckman-teamwork.doc

Bridgeland, J., DiIulio, J., & Wulsin, S. (2008). Engaged for Success: Service Learning as a Tool for Dropout Prevention. Civic Enterprises. Retrieved March 27, 2010 from http://docs.google.com/viewer?a=v&q=cache:Kf5pFlftonQJ:www.civicenterprises.net/pdfs/service-learning.pdf+http://www.civicenterprises.net/pdfs/service-learning.pdf&hl=en&gl=us&pid=bl&srcid=ADGEESiDstise8PZ7pYintaU5GbqmdGrSLgotHRnZKpTrrODebk4bulSaR3LxEl4bLG5Xf51GFVONZVKr9NqHJ7BwfyuF8DQX-HScTker6EkWc9SgOe5HM3UElXbS3NKN3Z39K6cHaYd&sig=AHIEtbQM_qgYUJ_B8-0bkqCQh0BoK50w0A.

Bridgeland, J., DiIulio, J., Jr., & Morison, K. (2006). The Silent Epidemic: Perspectives of High School Dropouts. Retrieved March 29, 2010 from http://www.civicenterprises.net/pdfs/thesilentepidemic3-06.pdf.

Curtis, D. (2001). Real World Issues Motivate Students. Edutopia. Retrieved March 29, 2010 from http://www.edutopia.org/start-pyramid.

David, J. (2009). Service Learning and Civic Participation. Association for Supervision and Curriculum Development. Retrieved April 24, 2010 from http://www.ascd.org/publications/educational_leadership/may09/vol66/num08/Service_Learning_and_Civic_Participation.aspx

Dewey, J. (1938). *Education and experience*. New York: Macmillan. Dewey, J. (2007). *Experience and education*. New York, NY: Simon and Schuster.

Edutopia, (2016). STEAM and Project based learning: real solutions from driving questions. Retrieved from https://www.edutopia.org/practice/steam-project-based-learning-real-solutions-driving-questions

Eccles, J. S., & Midgley, C. (1989). Stage-environment fit: Developmentally appropriate classrooms for young adolescents. *Research on motivation in education, 3*, 139-186.

Eccles J., Midgley C., Wigfield A., Buchanan C.M., Reuman D., Flanagan C., & Iver D.M. (1993). Development during adolescence. The impact of stage-environment fit on young adolescents' experiences in schools and in families. *American Psychology, 48*(2), 90-101.

Eyler, J., & D. E. Giles, J. (1999). Where's the Learning in Service-Learning? San Francisco: Jossey-Bass.

Farber, K. (2016a). *Entry events for project based learning*. Tarrant Institute for Innovative Education. Retrieved from http://tiie.w3.uvm.edu/blog/entry-events-for-project-based-learning/

Farber, K. (2016b). *Eight methods for reflection in project based learning*. Tarrant Institute for Innovative Education. Retrieved at http://tiie.w3.uvm.edu/blog/reflection-in-project-based-learning/-WGgfEbYrIn0

Farber, K. (2016c). Learn like a pirate: key takeaways. Tarrant Institute for InnovativeEducation. Retrieved at http://tiie.w3.uvm.edu/blog/learn-like-pirate/#.WMfrnBIrL_8

Farber, K. (2016d). The doing revolution: Service learning, early adolescents, and personal growth (Doctoral dissertation, NORTHEASTERN UNIVERSITY).

Farber, K. (2016e). *Three types of videos for showcasing content areas*. Tarrant Institute for Innovative Education. Retrieved at http://tiie.w3.uvm.edu/blog/videos-for-showcasing-content-areas/

Free Press Release Center (n.d.) Sample Press Release. Retrieved April 24, 2010 from http://www.free-press-release-center.info/sample-press-release.html

Freire, P. (1970). The banking concept of education. 2004) Educational foundations: An anthology of critical readings, 99-111.

Goldenring, J. M., & Rosen, D. S. (2004). Getting into adolescent heads: an essential update. *Contemporary Pediatrics , 21*(1), 64-92.

Greenfield, J (n.d.) Bringing Justice Home: First Steps Towards Community Action. Retrieved April 24, 2010 from http://bostonteachnet.org/greenfield/sigproj.htm

Hill, J. (2016). Makerspace wonderland at Crossett Brook MS. Retrieved from http://tiie.w3.uvm.edu/blog/the-story-of-Makerspace/#.WHJXfLYrL_8

Hopkins, D. (2008). Is Community Service a Waste of Time? Education World. Retrieved April 24, 2010 from http://www.educationworld.com/a_curr/curr188.shtml.

Humans of New York, (2016). Retrieved from http://www.humansofnewyork.com/

Kahne, J., Sporte, S. (2007). Developing Citizens: The Impact of Civic Learning Opportunities on Students' Commitment to Civic Participation. Consortium on Chicago School Research. Retrieved March 29, 2010 from http://www.eric.ed.gov/ERICWebPortal/custom/portlets/recordDetails/detailmini.jsp?_nfpb=true&_&ERICExtSearch_SearchValue_0=ED499374&ERICExtSearch_SearchType_0=no&accno=ED499374.

KIDS Consortium. (2005). Kids as Planners Guide Book. Lewiston, Maine.

Kohn, Alfie. (2002). Standardized Testing: Separating Wheat Children from Chaff Children. Excerpted from the foreword to Susan Ohanian's book What Happened to Recess and Why Are Our Children Struggling in Kindergarten? New York: McGraw-Hill, 2002.

Kolb, D. A. (1984). *Experiential learning: Experience as the source of learning and development*. New Jersey: Prentice Scales.

Larmer, Mergendoller, & Boss (2015). Setting the Standard for Project Based Learning. Alexandria, VA: ASCD.

Legeros, L. (2016). *5 ways to partner with students in a Makerspace.* Tarrant Institute of Innovative Education. Retrieved from http://tiie.w3.uvm.edu/blog/partner-with-students-in-a-Makerspace/

Legeros, L. (2016). *Brainado!* Tarrant Institute for Innovative Education. Retrieved from http://tiie.w3.uvm.edu/blog/brainado/

Makerspace (2013). The Makerspace playbook. Retrieved from http://makered.org/wp-content/uploads/2014/09/Makerspace-Playbook-Feb-2013.pdf

McCallumore, K., & Sparapani, E. F. (2010). The importance of the ninth grade on high school graduation rates and student success. *Education Digest, 76*(2), 60-64.

Managing Groups (n.d.). Teaching Effectiveness Program Academic Learning Service. University of Oregon. Retrieved from http://www.uoregon.edu/~tep/technology/blackboard/docs/groups.pdf on June 23, 2010.

Morgan, W. (1999). Standardized Test Scores Improve with Service Learning. Center for Participation and Citizenship at Indiana University, Bloomington. Retrieved March 20, 2010 from http://www.ri.net/middletown/mef/linksresources/documents/ServiceLearningBetterScores.pdf.

National Center for Education Statistics. (2010). Service-Learning and Community Service in K-12 Public Schools. Retrieved March 20, 2010 from http://nces.ed.gov/surveys/frss/publications/1999043/

National Center for Education Statistics. (1999). Fast Response Survey System; Fast Response Survey System, National Student Service-Learning and Community Service Survey. Retrieved March 20, 2010 from http://nces.ed.gov/quicktables/Detail.asp?Key=202.

National Commission on Service Learning. (2010). Learning in Deed, the Power of Service Learning for America's Schools. Retrieved March 20, 2010 from http://nslp.convio.net/site/DocServer/executive_summary.pdf?docID=1202

National Service Learning Clearinghouse. (2010). What is Service Learning? Retrieved March 20, 2010 from http://www.servicelearning.org/what-service-learning.

National Service Learning Clearinghouse, (2008). Why Districts, Schools and Classrooms Should Practice Service Learning. Retrieved March 20, 2010 From http://www.servicelearning.org/filemanager/download/two-page_fs/Why_Districts,_Schools,_and_Classrooms_Should_Practice_SL_FS_Short_Final_Mar08.pdf

Pennsylvania Service Learning Alliance. (2002-2007). Reflection: It's Easier than you Think. Retrieved May 5, 2010 from http://www.paservicelearning.org/Project_Ideas/Reflection.html

Pink (2016). The genius hour: how 60 minutes a week can electrify your job. Retrieved from http://www.danpink.com/2011/07/the-genius-hour-how-60-minutes-a-week-can-electrify-your-job/

Responsive Classroom, (2010). Our approach. Retrieved at https://www.responsiveclassroom.org/about.

Rich, B. (2016). Learning targets and learning scales. Retrieved from http://mtabelearning.weebly.com/learning-targets-and-learning-scales.html

Service Learning and Assessment: A Field Guide for Teachers. National Service-Learning and Assessment Study Group, October 1999. Retrieved May 2, 2010 from http://www.vermontcommunityworks.org/cwpublications/slassessguide/AssessGdChpt1-2.pdf.

Smink, J. & Reimer, M. (2005). Fifteen Strategies to Improve Attendance and Truancy Prevention. National Dropout Prevention Center. Retrieved March 27, 2010 from http://www.eric.ed.gov/ERICDocs/data/ericdocs2sql/content_storage_01/0000019b/80/1b/ac/a5.pdf.

Solarz, P. (2015). *Learn like a pirate.* Dave Burgess Consulting.

Steinke, P., & Fitch, P. (2007). Assessing Service-Learning. Research & Practice in Assessment. Volume 1, Issue 2, June 2007. Retrieved May 2, 2010 from http://www.virginiaassessment.org/rpa/2/Steinke%20Fitch.pdf.

University of Minnesota, (2016). Reflection in service learning classes. Retrieved from http://www.servicelearning.umn.edu/info/reflection.html

University of Southern California (2010). History of Service Learning. Retrieved July 25, 2010 from http://college.usc.edu/history-of-service-learning/

References

Vygotsky, L. S. (1997). The Collected Works of LS Vygotsky: Problems of the theory and history of psychology (Vol. 3). New York, NY: Springer Science & Business Media.

Zvi, G. & Krebs, D., (2016). Genius hour definition. Retrieved from http://www.geniushourguide.org/heres-our-short-definition-of-genius-hour/

About the Author

Katy Farber is currently a professional development coordinator at the University of Vermont in the Tarrant Institute for Innovative Education. She works with Vermont teachers to innovate and personalize education, writes and speaks frequently about educational change and progress, and collaborates with colleagues to create professional development resources and educational research.

Katy completed seventeen years of public school teaching in central Vermont at the middle- and upper-elementary level. She served as a teacher mentor, service-learning consultant, and teacher leader in her district. Katy was Vermont's Teacher of the Year alternate in 2014.

Katy's first book, *Why Great Teachers Quit and How We Can Stop the Exodus*, was published in July 2010 by Corwin Press. The first edition of this book, called *Change the World with Service Learning: How to Organize, Lead, and Assess Service Learning Projects*, was published in early 2011. In May 2016, Katy graduated from Northeastern University with a doctorate of education in curriculum, teaching, learning, and leadership. Her dissertation was a case study about the impact of service learning on early adolescent students' personal growth.

Katy lives in Vermont with her husband and two daughters.